Management Sage

Leadership Skills

Management Sage

Leadership Skills

First Step Publishing
Paving Ways For New Writers

First Published in India in 2016 by First Step Publishing

First Edition 2016

Editorial / Sales / Marketing Office at
303-304 Garnet Nirmal Lifestyles Ph 2
Behind Nirmal Lifestyles Mall
LBS Marg Mulund West
Mumbai 400080
E-Mail:- info@firststepcorp.com
www.firststepcorp.com

ISBN: - 978-93-83306-33-6
Publisher: First Step Publishing
Branding, Marketing and Promotions by: Design Fishing
Digital Management by: First Step Corp
Cover Design:. Design Fishing
Typeset in Book Antique
Price: $ 40

Table Of Content

Preface

The best leadership style for any particular team will be influenced by its purpose and composition. This eBook provides a practical guide to understanding team dynamics to help you with practical day-to-day team building.

You will learn:

- How the study of group dynamics can be applied to real-world team building issues.
- The five factors you must put in place to ensure that the team's dynamics remain positive and productive.
- How to recognize the development stages that a new team must undergo before reaching its full potential.
- Why you should modify your level of involvement depending upon which stage your team is at.
- How conflict affects your team members why you need to coach them in developing their own coping strategies.

Introduction

A great deal of research has been published on team building and team dynamics. Even though most of this research is purely academic and has been performed in a research environment rather than in the workplace, some of it does contain value for a working manager.

In particular, there have been two studies that you should be familiar with: Bruce Tuckman's `Stages for a Group' and Richard Hackman's `Five Factor Model.' This eBook describes both of these in detail and explains how they can help you with practical day-today team building and team management.

How one defines a team varies according to the context one is referring to, but it is useful to look at three widely accepted definitions:

1. A team is a] group in which members work together intensively to achieve a common group goal. (Lewis-McClear & Taylor, 1998)
2. A team is a small number of people with complementary skills who are committed to a common purpose, performance goals, and approach for which they are mutually accountable. (Katzenbach & Smith, 1993)
3. A team is made up of people] working together in a committed way to achieve a common goal or mission. The work is interdependent and team members share responsibility and hold themselves accountable for attaining the results.' (MIT Information Services and Technology, 2007)

The common thread in each of these definitions is that teams consist of a group of people who share a common understanding of their goal and work together to accomplish it.

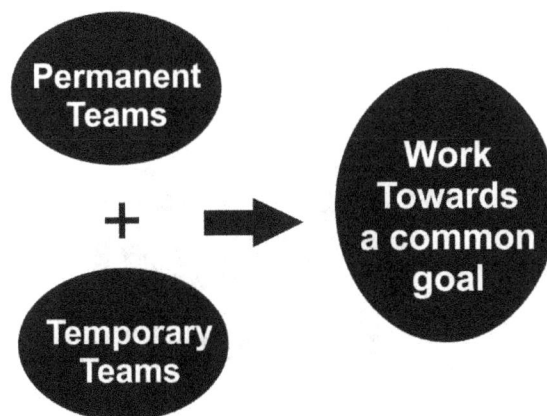

None of these definitions states whether the team is a fixed or transient entity, yet in the world of work there are many examples of both permanent and temporary teams:

- A temporary group could be brought together to:
  - Investigate or solve a specific issue
  - Design a new product or service
  - Act as a committee to resolve an issue

- A permanent group could be formed:
  - To act as a steering committee
  - With responsibility for a particular function
  - From the same functional area who meet regularly to seek work improvement opportunities

Whilst the purpose of the team may be described as permanent in the examples above it is inevitable that the membership of this type of team will change over time.

This will be for a variety of reasons: for example, individual members, including the leader, may leave or be replaced; those with a scarce skill may be seconded to another team that is in greater need of their skills; or a team's composition will change, even if the purpose remains, when an organization is taken over by or merged with another.

The support structure you have at your disposal will directly affect the success of your team, and your ability to reward, develop, and inform your team members will play a significant part in your team's and your own success.

Whether you are managing a temporary or permanent team there are considerable benefits successful teams bring to organizations.

Benefits of teams:
More productive
Deliver larger projects
Bring together expertise
Build a 'community'

Many projects in the workplace are too large or complex for one individual to complete and the use of teams ensures the project's timely success. This is especially true of IT development projects and organization-wide projects.

Perhaps one of the most important benefits a team can provide is that of increased and broader-based expertise when compared to an individual. One person on their own will not have all the necessary skills to deliver a product or service.

Teams comprise individuals with complementary knowledge that can far exceed that of a single person. Team members are also able to coordinate their efforts in order to produce the desired outcome on schedule and to budget.

Through specialist teams and steering committees departments can combine their knowledge to take an active role in company-wide and strategic-level decisions. This helps these divisions and departments to feel they have some `ownership' of the decisions made when the board acts upon these recommendations.

This `ownership' reinforces the organizational community feeling. This community sentiment permeates throughout the organization and is often the motivation for calling a group of people a team. An example of this is a Customer Support Team where individuals share the same set of skills and all do exactly the same job, thus having a collective expertise within the team.

By creating this type of team environment management boosts the morale of both the individual and the workplace. This does not mean all groups of people performing the same role are referred to as a team (e.g. the accounts department), but they have their group identity, and morale is based on their department's contribution to the organization.

Key Points

- ✓ A team is a group of people who share a common understanding of their mission and work together to accomplish it.
- ✓ Teams can be temporary or permanent.
- ✓ Managing a team will reflect the nature and composition of that team.
- ✓ Your ability to manage and motivate teams under your authority will have a significant correlation with your career aspirations.
    - ✓ Teams bring several benefits to organizations:
    - ✓ Greater levels and depth of expertise.
    - ✓ More productive than individuals.
    - ✓ Able to deliver large projects successfully.
    - ✓ Build a workplace community, thus boosting morale.

Bruce Tuckman's 'Stages for a Group'

Much of the theory of team building is based on academic research and has its roots in both psychology and sociology. It began with the work of Wilhelm Wundt (1832-1920), who is credited as the founder of experimental psychology. It was Kurt Lewin (1890-1947), a social psychologist, who coined the phrase `group dynamics' to describe the positive and negative forces within groups of people.

In 1945, Lewin established The Group Dynamics Research Center at the Massachusetts Institute of Technology, the first institute devoted explicitly to the study of group dynamics and how it could be applied to real-world, social issues.

As research continued in this area throughout the second half of the twentieth century its focus moved more into studying how group performance could be improved in the workplace.

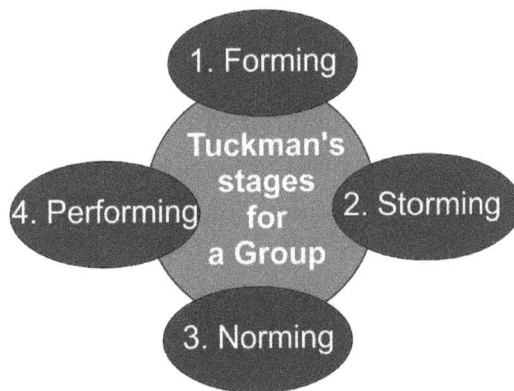

One of the most influential studies in this area is Bruce Tuckman's (1965). He proposed the four-stage model called `Tuckman's Stages for a Group,' which states that the ideal group decision-making process should occur in four stages:

1. Forming
2. Storming
3. Norming
4. Performing

Tuckman maintained that these phases are all necessary and inevitable in order for the team to grow, to face up to challenges, to tackle problems, to find solutions, to plan work, and to deliver results.

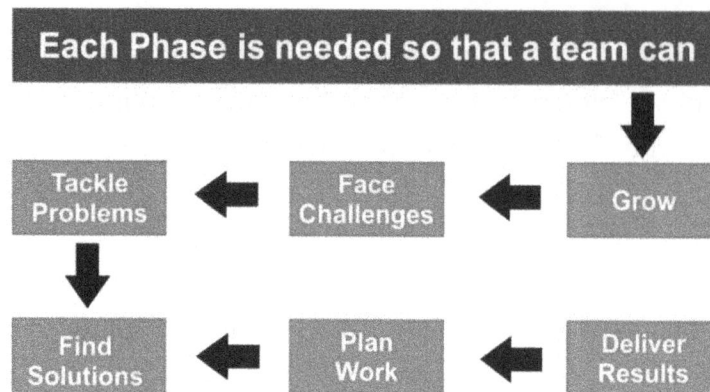

Each Phase is needed so that a team can

Tackle Problems ← Face Challenges ← Grow

Find Solutions ← Plan Work ← Deliver Results

This model has become the basis for subsequent models and it is important to understand the process of each stage and its concepts so that you can apply it to your workplace.

Stage 1--Forming

This first stage involves the bringing together of a group of individuals to form a team. At this stage, members usually have positive expectations about the venture, although they may harbour some anxiety about other members, such as who they are and what they are like.

At this point it is about building relationships within the group and clarifying the team's mission. Initially individuals behave independently of each other, but as they gather information and impressions about:

- Each other,
- The scope of the task,
- Its challenges and opportunities, and
- How to approach it the team members begin to agree on goals and tackle particular tasks.

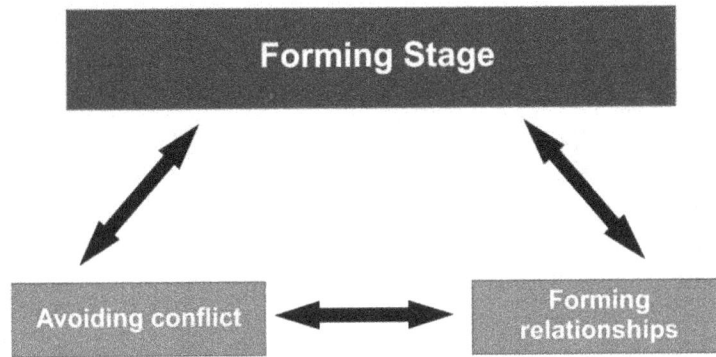

Each individual's behaviour is driven by a desire to be accepted by the other team members and to avoid conflict. This results in serious issues being avoided, or put off, as team members concentrate on non-contentious or routine issues.

This reluctance to engage in and resolve areas of conflict means that the team accomplishes very little and the underlying differences which have been brushed aside will eventually surface and have to be addressed.

The length of this first stage will depend on how clearly the task is defined and on how much experience the individuals have of working in a team. Groups with simple tasks will move through orientation quickly, but groups with complex goals and tasks may spend much longer in this stage.

Teams made up of people who are used to being autonomous will take longer to build the necessary relationships for a successful team than those used to working in a group. Many individuals may be reluctant to contribute at this stage and their support of the leader is given cautiously.

As a manager you need to be very `hands on' at this stage, giving clear directions and structure to make sure that your team build strong relationships. You can facilitate this by making sure your communications dispel any misunderstandings that could arise about roles and responsibilities.

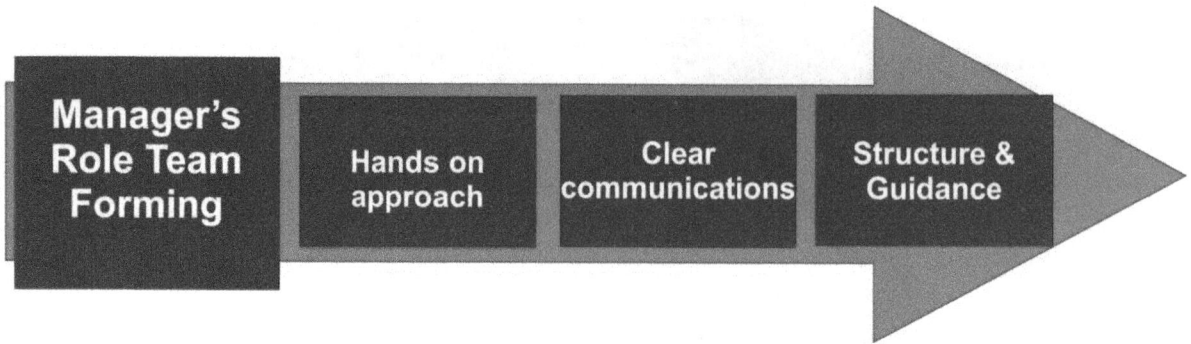

| Manager's Role Team Forming | Hands on approach | Clear communications | Structure & Guidance |

With decisions being made in the majority of cases by the nominated leader you also need to ensure that no team member is committing themselves to do too much, or too little, of the planned work.

By paying attention from the outset to building good relationships, as well as focusing on a clearly defined task, your team will perform better than teams whose managers rush through or skip over the relationship-building stage.

Stage 2--Storming

During this second stage, where team members feel more able to express and question opinions, you will see more evidence of internal conflict. Your role as manager is to contain and direct this energy into a productive channel. You need to be aware that some level of internal conflict will cause a simultaneous dip in team morale.

Your management role will have to become more supportive, guiding the team in their decision-making and offering explanations of how these decisions came about. You need to define what you and the organization expect of the team in terms of professional behaviour.

This more instructional approach will enable you, as team manager, to prevent any conflict from getting out of control and poisoning relationships between team members.

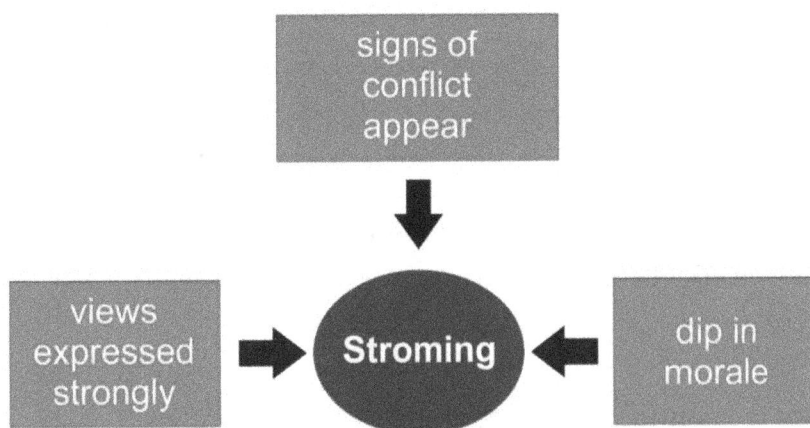

You will be able to recognize when your team moves into the `storming' stage because you will observe your team beginning to address the differences between their initial perceptions and the reality of the situation that they have been formed to address. This will cover issues such as what problems they are really supposed to solve, how they will function independently and together, and what leadership model they will accept.

As your team members begin to negotiate the work assignments and express their views on the best way to achieve the task outcome disagreements will arise. Through your active listening skills you will mediate and help decisions to be made through compromise as the most efficient way to attain the necessary outcomes.

While your team members confront each other's ideas, test differing perspectives, discuss what the group needs to do, and how best to accomplish it, your role becomes one of a facilitator building trust within sub-groups of the team.

Team storming, whilst it may be contentious and unpleasant, will be resolved relatively quickly with your guidance and support. You must view this as a necessary step for your team to become a cohesive whole, not as an enormous irritation to be dismissed.

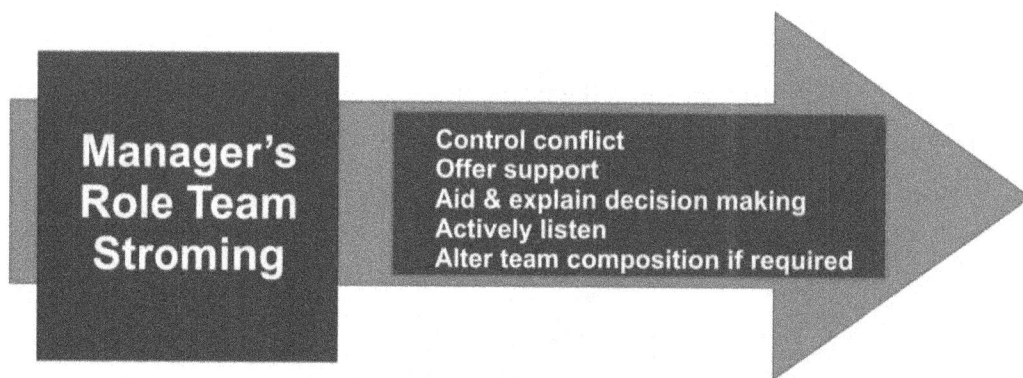

Manager's Role Team Stroming

Control conflict
Offer support
Aid & explain decision making
Actively listen
Alter team composition if required

As a manager you need to be mindful of how this `conflict' affects your team members and coach them in developing their own coping strategies. For example, some individuals may:

- Find this stage painful because they are averse to conflict.
- Feel anger or frustration with the task or with other members.
- Resent the presence of formal leadership.
- Focus on minutiae to avoid the real issues confronting the team.

The maturity in terms of attitude and approach to problem resolution of some team members can be significant in determining whether your team will ever move out of this stage.

If you try to bulldoze through this stage in your team's development you may find it becomes a permanent state, resulting in low morale and lack of productivity. If you fear this is happening to your team you will need to see how much flexibility you have in altering the composition of your team within the constraints of your organization.

You may choose to break the team into smaller subsets of cohesive individuals within your team so that morale and productivity are raised.

Stage 3--Norming

Once your team has reached the third stage of its development the members focus on resolving differences so that the mission and goals can be clearly defined. Your role within the team transfers from that of leader to that of team member.

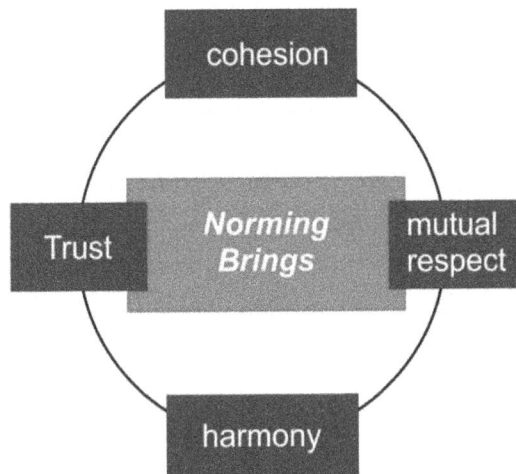

Team members are learning more about each other and how they will work together and are developing tools such as a problem-solving process, a code of conduct, a set of team values, and measurement indicators. The team has now established core processes, and as manager you need to ensure the team avoids spending unnecessary time on issues related to the smaller processes.

During this period of negotiation and discussion, your role becomes one of observer and facilitator in order to assist your team in establishing the ground rules of behaviour as they learn to work together. Their attitudes are characterized by decreasing animosities toward other members; feelings of cohesion, mutual respect, harmony, and trust; and a feeling of pleasure in accomplishing tasks.

19

Your team is truly developing a sense of team pride, and you will see evidence of increased productivity as skills develop. The team arrive at decisions that are more in line with their purpose rather than from a position of compromise.

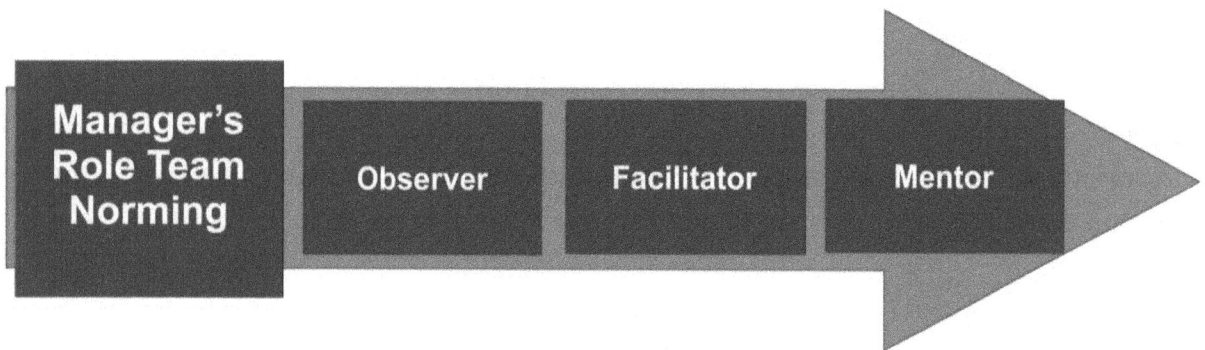

Manager's Role Team Norming → Observer → Facilitator → Mentor →

You can begin to transform your role as coach to one of a mentor and delegator, offering your team greater opportunities to raise their levels of expertise.

Stage 4--Performing

Now your team has reached the final stage of its development and can now bring real benefits to you and the organization. Your team members are now competent, autonomous, and able to handle the decision-making process without supervision.

Your team has been accomplishing work at every stage, but it is at this `performing' stage that work is accomplished most effectively. Morale is high and the general atmosphere is positive. Team members' attitudes are characterized by positive feelings and eagerness to be part of the team.

Members are confident about the outcome, enjoy open communication, exhibit high energy, and disagreement is expected and allowed as long as it is channelled through means acceptable to the team. Leadership within the team is often shared and tasks are delegated within the team, which makes the overall decision-making process operate more easily than at earlier stages.

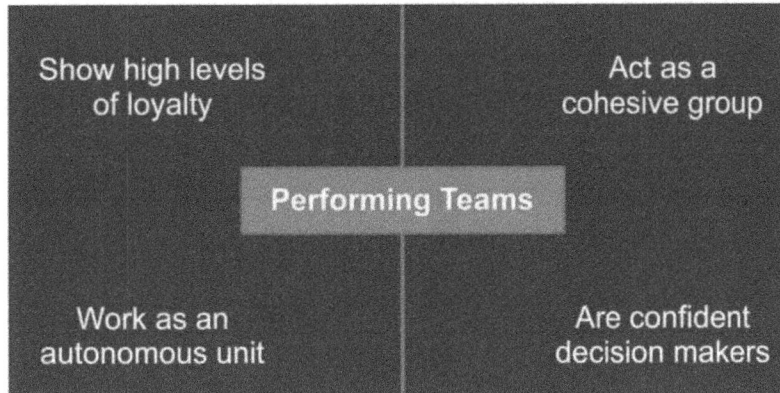

As a manager, once your team is operating at this level then your role becomes one of overseer and delegator. You are no longer involved in day-to-day activities and the team's relationships with each other emulate the high degree of trust and loyalty you show in your relationship with the team.

Another key task you will perform at this stage is one of monitoring your team's relationships and performance to ensure that the group dynamics remain positive and productive. This is because changes in the dynamics of the group can result in high-performing teams reverting to earlier team-building stages.

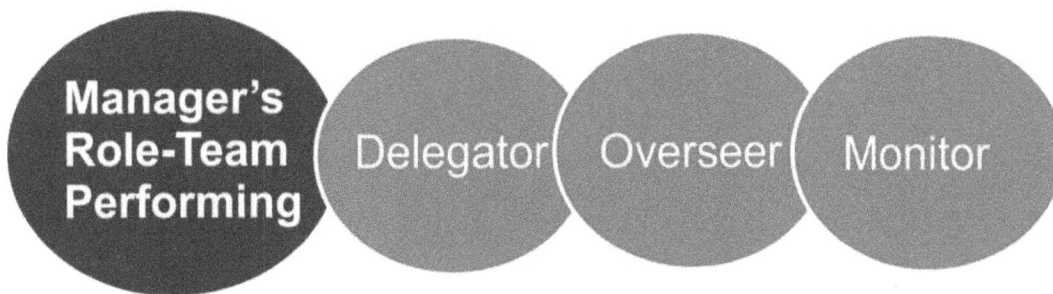

For example, a change in leadership may cause the team to revert to `storming' as the new people challenge the existing norms and dynamics of the team.

Whilst Tuckman's model has been extremely influential in terms of improving peoples' understanding of how group dynamics change as a team becomes a cohesive group, it is not readily transferable to the world of work.

In the more than fifty years since Tuckman's research many others have related group dynamics to the place of work. It is the model of J. Richard Hackman that is frequently referred to when one is responsible for designing and managing work groups.

Richard Hackman's `Five Factor Model'

In 2002, whilst working at Harvard, Richard Hackman developed a research-based model for designing and managing work groups.

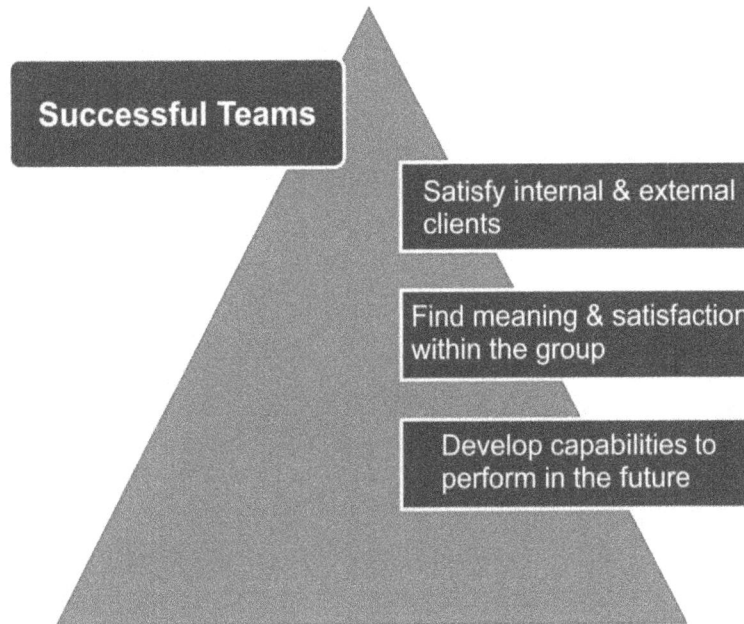

Successful Teams

Satisfy internal & external clients

Find meaning & satisfaction within the group

Develop capabilities to perform in the future

His research looked at why some groups were successful and what it was that made them so. He identified three attributes that such groups possessed:

- They satisfy internal and external clients,
- They develop capabilities to perform in the future, and
- The members find meaning and satisfaction within the group.

He then went on to identify the conditions that can increase the chances of success for teams. This he called his `Five Factor Model.'

<u>*Those five factors are:*</u>

1. Being a Real Team
2. Compelling Direction
3. Enabling Structure
4. Supportive Context
5. Expert Coaching

These phrases need to be defined so that you can see how in your management role you can influence the success of your team by ensuring these elements exist within the environment of your department.

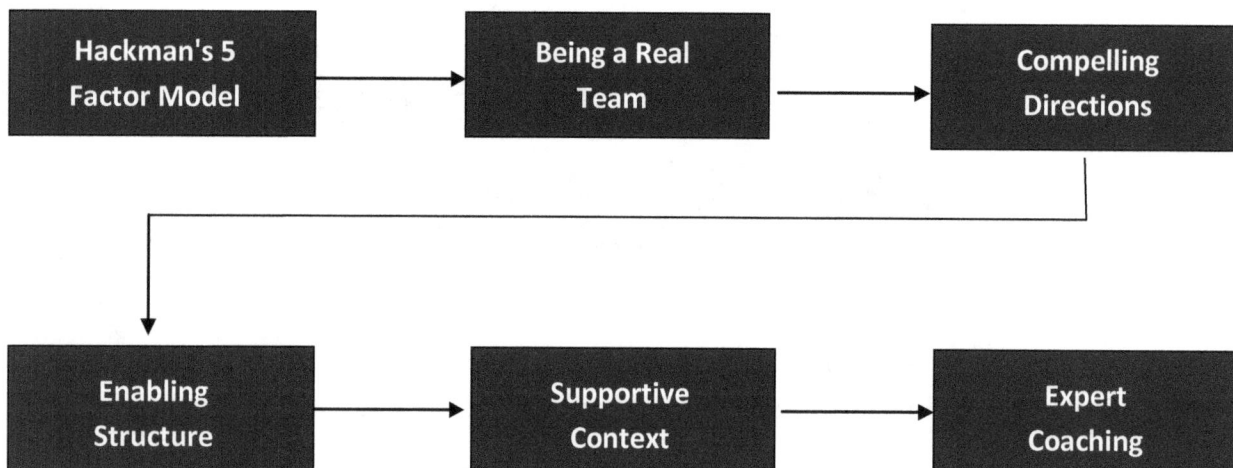

```
┌──────────────┐      ┌──────────────┐      ┌──────────────┐
│ Hackman's 5  │ ───▶ │ Being a Real │ ───▶ │ Compelling   │
│ Factor Model │      │    Team      │      │ Directions   │
└──────────────┘      └──────────────┘      └──────────────┘

┌──────────────┐      ┌──────────────┐      ┌──────────────┐
│  Enabling    │ ───▶ │ Supportive   │ ───▶ │   Expert     │
│  Structure   │      │  Context     │      │  Coaching    │
└──────────────┘      └──────────────┘      └──────────────┘
```

<u>*Factor 1--Being a Real Team*</u>

What does Hackman mean by `being a real team'? The elements he said were required to ensure your team is `a real team' are: the members have a shared task, the team boundaries clearly state who is inside or outside of the group, and the group membership is stable.

As a manager you will have direct control over the first two elements of what constitutes `a real team', but it is the stability of the group members that is often the hardest aspect to control. If you are based in a project-type environment then it is probable that team stability will last only as long as the project.

If your team includes someone with a rare skill, even this level of stability may not be possible, as different project teams may vie for this scarce resource.

Instability within the team composition can also arise from the nature of the work. For example, managing within a call centre environment is often plagued by a high rate of staff turnover due to the nature of the job and the fact that it often attracts transient individuals.

As a manager in this type of environment you will be able to minimize the inevitable disruption of staff turnover by developing an induction program that quickly integrates new recruits into the team.

Factor 2--Compelling Direction

The second factor of this model is that of providing you team with a compelling direction. This means that you provide your team with clear goals, which are both challenging and consequential.

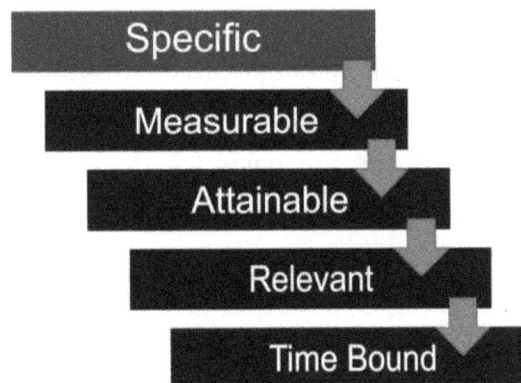

As a manager, whatever type of team you are responsible for, you have direct control over the goals you set your team. You can also ensure that you set SMART goals for your staff that motivate and reward them.

These goals need to clearly state how the team contributes to the organization so that the team is aware of their own contribution to the overall mission.

Factor 3--Enabling Structure

The structure that your team exists in is the third factor that Hackman cites as influential in making your team a success. Some of these aspects you will have control over, while others are going to be dictated by the type of organization you are in and your role within it

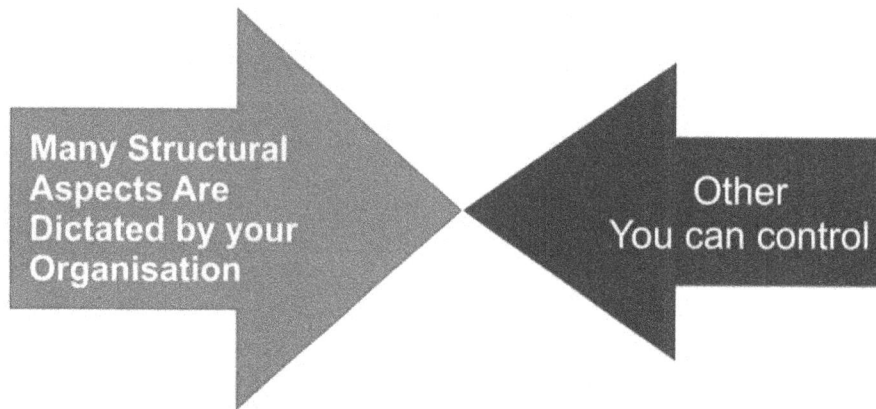

Where possible, offering your team variety in the tasks they must complete improves the team's success. Examples might include small changes in task assignment if you are managing a call center team, or keeping the size of your team at a manageable level so that they are not too large and become unwieldy. Sometimes you may want to make small sub-groups within a large team so that the qualities of successful teams can be nurtured.

Within your team's structure you will also want to ensure that some of your key players have good social skills. This makes certain that persuasion and well-presented arguments rather than conflict forms the basis for decision making within the team. These social skills will also ensure that behaviour is guided by strong norms.

Factor 4--Supportive Context

The fourth quality required to ensure successful teams is that of support. A supportive context is essential for companies and organizations, as they are made up of small groups which when combined form a larger group.

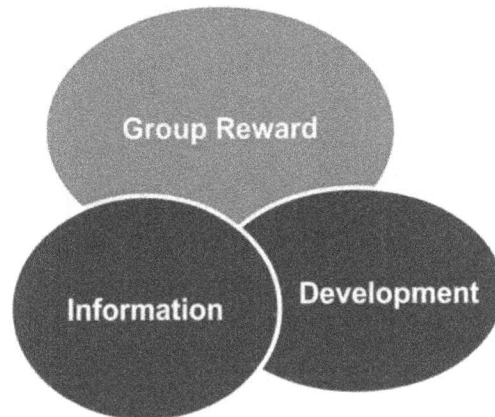

This support framework is made up of three elements: reward, development, and information. The reward must be linked to the performance of the group or team. This system must be based upon rewarding the group's performance and cooperation.

The second element of the support must be the development of individual members' skills through an educational system. For many organizations this educational system is formed around the Appraisal System, and as a manager it is vital that you develop your skills in this area.

The third supportive element is connected to the provision of information and guaranteeing easy access to this data and materials. Your ability as a manager to ensure your team have access to the information and materials they need to develop their own skills is crucial.

You can take advantage of the advances in communications technology (computers, notebooks, eBook readers, and smartphones, etc.) and the Internet. You will be able to guide your team to the best resources and information they require to develop their skills.

Factor 5--Expert Coaching

This guidance leads into the finally aspect of the Five Factor Model, that of expert coaching and mentoring. Through the annual appraisal system and your day-to-day management of the team you are able to identify which members of your team require your help with a task, or help that individual develop their interpersonal skills.

Once this need has been identified you coach the person in how they can best meet this challenge and develop the skills they lack. You must be conscious not to be too overbearing in your manner, as this can seriously undermine the effectiveness of the team. The latter is a criticism that Hackman draws attention to in his research and it will significantly reduce the success of any team.

Hackman has been publishing work on teams since 1967 and his work in this area remains highly regarded. Many of the academic papers written by Hackman are available
at: http://www.people.fas.harvard.edu/~hackman/csvsearch.cgi?search=hackman

Most teams you encounter in the working world are likely to exhibit a mix of Tuckman's Four Stages and Hackman's Five Factor Model in their day-to-day operations.

As a manager it is useful to be able to identify the stage at which your group is operating and which of the five factors are present in your organization. By understanding the group dynamics of your team in this way you are better able to adapt your leadership style and behaviors to suit your current team.

You will encounter teams that are an almost permanent fixture, but in which individual members may come and go. Your role in this instance is to ensure that any new members are integrated into the pre-existing team as quickly as possible. This enables the team to continue to operate most effectively.

Other teams are more temporary in nature, often set up for a specific project. Frequently this type of team will be made up of individuals who are familiar with and have a great deal of experience of working in teams.

If you are managing this type of team you will facilitate the team to be a cohesive unit as they are likely to be very clear about each other's responsibilities. This means that the forming and storming stages will be more quickly resolved as the whole team is focused
on its objective.

As your career progresses you will inherit teams with each new position, and being able to identify at which stage of development this new team is at will help you provide the correct level of support and guidance.

It is inevitable that at some point in your career you will come across a dysfunctional team that is locked into the storming stage and is unwilling to progress no matter what you do. In some instances the only way to handle such a team is to create sub-teams within this group so that each can work effectively and productively.

You can also ensure that the team environment is conducive to the attainment of goals and that sufficient support is available to individuals, with the addition of your coaching expertise as and when required.

Key Points

- ✓ Tuckman'sfour-stagemodelstatesthattheidealgroupdecision-makingprocess should occur in four stages:

    1. forming,
    2. storming,
    3. norming, and
    4. performing.

- ✓ You can use this four-stage model to assist you in clearly identifying the group dynamics of your team.
- ✓ The four-stage model provides a framework for how you can best interact with your team.

- ✓ Hackman's model suggests that groups are successful when they:
    - ✓ Satisfy internal and external clients,
    - ✓ Develop capabilities to perform in the future, and

✓ Provide meaning and satisfaction in the group.

✓ Setting your team and its members SMART goals will ensure that they have a clear focus for their activities.
✓ Developing your appraisal management skills will enable you to ensure an appropriate team structure and provide a supportive environment in which your team can develop their ownskills.

Summary

Team working provides a wide variety of benefits to organizations from bringing together diverse expertise to building a workplace community. This makes it very difficult to generalize about teams as even within the same organization there will be teams that have very little in common.

The best management style for any particular team will be influenced by its purpose and composition. This means that you will have to think carefully about each piece of team building or team management advice that you encounter. You will need to ask yourself, under what conditions would this be helpful, be of limited use, or be completely inappropriate?

Remember, your ability to manage and motivate teams under your authority will have a significant correlation with your career aspirations because team leadership is such an essential skill in the modern workplace.

Preface

Successful team building in the workplace has more to do with making a success of the team you have been given, rather than building an ideal team from scratch. There are certain core principles of team building that will help you get the best out of any team that you find yourself managing.

You will learn how to apply these principles to:
- A project team where even though you are not an expert in all of the technical aspects of the project you are still expected to coordinate the team's efforts.
- A support team where there are problems with motivation and high staff turnover.
- A high-level strategic team where you do not have any direct authority over the other participants.

Introduction

You will probably have been a member of several teams during your life--for example, a sports team, theatre group, church group, bridge club, etc. As a result, you should already have some understanding of how teams function and what motivates them to be successful.

As useful as this knowledge is, it is worth pointing out some of the differences between these types of non-work teams and those teams that you will need to manage as part of your job.

Firstly, teams that are outside of a working environment are usually made up of people who have a common set of beliefs and have actively chosen to join. Secondly, the team objective will be clear and universally agreed. Thirdly, anyone who does not fit in with the group will tend to leave of their own accord. Finally, in the case of a sports team, the captain canfield the best players and leave the rest on the bench.

Things are very different with workplace teams.

As a manager you will often be presented with a team to manage which may or may not have a track record of success. Some of the team members may be enthusiastic, but some may not. People who don't fit in or who don't agree with the goals of the team may be reluctant to leave and it may be impossible to get rid of them. In addition, the people in your team are unlikely to have a common motivator as each one is influenced by their
own personal career aspirations. Sometimes, the goals that the team has been set may be either impossible to achieve or inappropriate.

Despite all of these constraints, there are certain core principles of team building that will help you get the best out of any team that you find yourself managing.

This Book explores three very different teams and describes how the principles of team building can be applied to each one. These example teams have been chosen because they represent the three most common types of team in the modern workplace.

The first example is typical of a multi-disciplinary project team that has been assembled to complete a particular piece of work. In this example, the team leader does not have total managerial control over all of the team members, which is normal with this type of team.

The second example is typical of a team that is performing an ongoing business process, in this case telephone support. In this example, the issues facing the team leader have more to do with maintaining team morale than with the work itself, which is reasonably straightforward.

The third example is typical of a team that is engaged in strategic planning. In this example, none of the team members report directly to the team leader and the goals of the team are changing all the time.

The issues facing the leader of each of these teams are discussed in detail. Even if your team does not match one of these scenarios exactly, there are still certain principles that will apply to your own team and it is up to you to interpret how best to apply them.

A Note About Team Leadership

The most important part of leading a team in the modern workplace is to be the person that others choose to follow. Even where compulsion is possible, it tends not to work very well. If you want to take a leadership role, then the most important questions you can ask are:

Which leadership style is the most appropriate to my team?
How can I alter my behaviours to become this type of leader?

The answers to these questions depend on your role, your team, and the task at hand. This aspect of team leadership is covered in the Book `Team Leadership Styles,' part of Management Sage Series.

Principles of Team Building

There has been a lot of academic study of teams and team building over the years and much of it has found its way into team building books aimed at managers. As a result, there are certain aspects of team building that have gained the status of `Golden Rules' that you should follow in order to build and manage a successful team.

A good example of this is team size. Academic studies have shown that the ideal team size is between five and nine, with six being the ideal number.

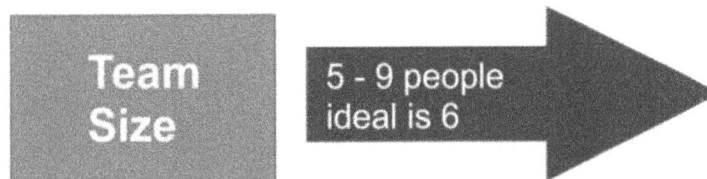

Team Size — 5 - 9 people ideal is 6

The effect of team size on productivity can be traced back to the work of Maximilian Ringelmann, a French agricultural engineer born in 1861. He discovered that the more people who pulled on a rope, the less effort each individual contributed, despite the total force generated by the group rising.

This effect became obvious after there were about five people on the rope. Ringelmann attributed this to what he called `social loafing.' This happens because working as part of a group or team tends to obscure the lack of individual effort.

The impact of social loafing is more significant where each team member is performing exactly the same mundane task. With this type of task it is very difficult for anyone to tell how much effort any one individual is putting in and very difficult to reward an individual, or give that person a sense of achievement. Not surprisingly, this results in individuals putting in as little effort as they think they can get away with.

As well as Ringelmann's work, there have been innumerable studies involving teambuilding programs and a large number of companies that have designed games specifically to test the factors affecting team cohesion, trust, and cooperation as well as the quality of the work done by various teams. The ideal team size to achieve the objectives set by these exercises seems to be around five or six.

This evidence does appear to be slightly more compelling than the Ringelmann experiment, but you should remember that the tasks set in this type of exercise are often designed with a fairly small group in mind. This leads to the circular logic that:

`Tasks designed to be completed by small groups are most efficiently completed by small groups.'

No doubt many of these academic studies have been performed rigorously and the results and findings are both valid and enlightening. Unfortunately, they are of little use to a manager or team leader working in the real world, where team size is usually something over which the manager has little control.

The reality for most team leaders and project managers is that the team size is dictated by the amount of work to be done and the time available. In a cross-functional project team, the size of the team is dictated by the functions that need to be represented. In either case, 95% of the time you will need to make the best of the team that you are given because the size and composition is something that you will not have much control over.

Similarly, you may have very little control over team rewards because some of the team members may not be under your direct control, remuneration may be decided at a higher management level, or you may be constrained by organizational policy.

All of this means that successful team building in the workplace has more to do with applying some basic principles to the team you have been given, rather than recruiting `perfect' team members in order to build an ideal team from scratch.

The four principles of team building are:

Define Success Criteria

The first principle is to define and communicate the team objective. This should be easily understood by everyone and allow all members to contribute, regardless of their skills and experience.

For a project team, success criteria will be defined in the project plan and it will be obvious on a week-by-week basis whether or not the project is on track. In addition, team members will be able to compare their progress with their individual work schedule. This means that project teams seldom have problems in this particular area.

However, with other types of team, the objective is not always so clear and team members who feel as though they do not have a definite objective can easily become de-motivated. There may also be a problem if the success criteria have been set at unrealistic levels and the team cannot `buy into' them. This often happens when people who do not appreciate the day-to-day realities of the task have set the goals. This is illustrated later
in this eBook with reference to one of the example teams.

Remember, success cannot be achieved unless the team actually knows what it looks like.

Lead by Example

In many instances, your team members will have more technical knowledge and more experience than you do. This is not a problem: leadership has more to do with `soft skills' than technical ones. Having said that, you may need some technical skills--for example, knowledge of a project management methodology if you are running a project team. However, no amount of technical expertise will make up for poor leadership skills.

Leading by example means exhibiting the same professional behaviours to everyone you interact with, whether they are inside or outside your team. This includes customers and suppliers as well as other people within your organization.

It can be tempting to allow your frustration with people outside the team to show in your comments or body language during team meetings and in conversations with individual team members. You should always make a concerted effort not to show a lack of respect in this way, even if you feel it is justified.

Demonstrating the type of behaviours you expect from your team in your own interactions communicates your expectations of how your team members should behave towards you and everyone else they come into contact with. If you can ensure that everyone on your team demonstrates respect towards customers, suppliers, and others who are not part of the team then this can prevent a lot of problems from taking root. There is always a tendency for teams to blame problems on those outside of the team and to ignore their own responsibilities. This is made easier for the team if there is an existing `us and them' sentiment.

As part of your time management ensure that you allocate time to communicate and monitor your team informally. For example, on your way back from getting a coffee, ask members of your team how things are going and listen carefully to their responses. Listen for omissions and look for negative body language. Many potential problems can be caught early by paying attention to what team members do not say as well as what they do say.

By utilizing both formal and informal contact time with your team you will be more likely to pick up on underlying issues and resolve them before they become serious.

Value All Contributions

Many teams will be significantly larger than the ideal of five to nine people, which can make it difficult to recognize each person's contribution.
You will need to show that you value each member of the team and that their views matter to you regardless of the role they play. One simple way to exhibit this is by ensuring all views are heard when talking about issues at a team meeting or discussion.

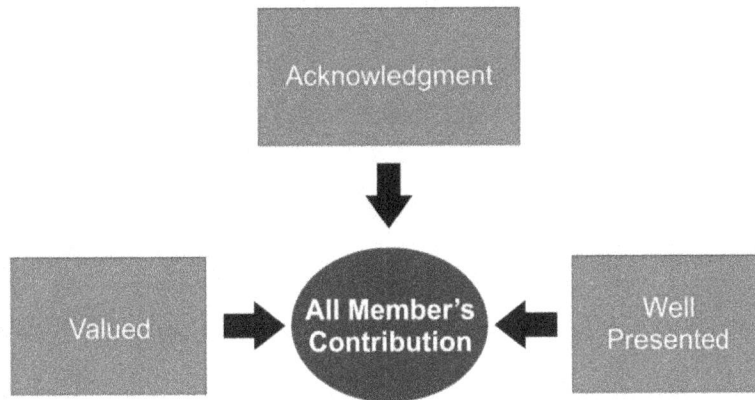

You should use your `Chair' skills during these events to ensure that everyone who wants to voice an opinion feels as though they will get a fair hearing. When people feel as though their opinions are unwelcome the most common response is to withdraw from the discussion and then seek out others who feel the same way. This leads to the formation of cliques and sub-groups that can be difficult to deal with once they have formed. The best way to prevent this type of team fragmentation is to make sure that everyone feels involved.

Reward Group Success

As a manager, you will usually have the ability to reward those team members you are directly responsible for. However, the extent to which you are able to offer truly motivating rewards, especially monetary, will be influenced by your organization's culture and the amount of decision-making power you have.

There may be some team members who are not part of the organization (e.g. contract or freelance staff). In these cases you will need to think carefully about how to reward their efforts in a meaningful way. One way of doing this is to make it clear that you will try to help them to secure more work from your organization. Most contractors and freelancers place a high value on continuity of employment and would consider being recommended for other projects within your organization as the equivalent of a monetary reward.

Whilst these things are helpful in terms of each individual, it offers no opportunity for you as the manager to reward the whole team. As the complexity and diversity of organizations increase many organizations are beginning to make provisions for team-based rewards, but this is still far from normal.

Recognise ➡ **Your Team** ⬅ **Reward**

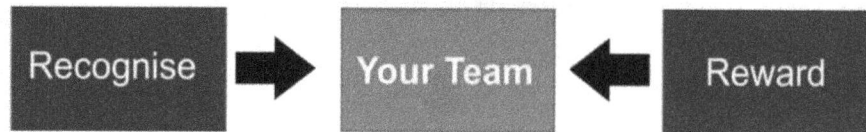

In situations where you are unable to offer a tangible reward you will have to seek ways to recognize the contribution and efforts of your team. This recognition can take many forms and can be large or small in relation to the achievement:

- Specific mention in your management report that you read to them.
- Mention of your team's achievement at the next divisional meeting. (This may mean for some teams that not everyone will be present on such an occasion, but the members will know that their efforts have been accredited.)
- Persuading a board member, senior customer contact, or someone they respect to acknowledge the team's contribution in an email or report, or if appropriate a visit to the team.
- Personal praise for the whole team in recognition of its efforts from you as their manager.
- Organize a social event. This can be as simple as taking everyone out for a meal at lunchtime. The amount of money you spend is far less important than the fact that you do `something' even if it is fairly low-key.

It is important that the recognition is in proportion to the achievement attained, otherwise it will be seen as arbitrary and could have a negative effect on the morale of the team as a whole.

Key Points

- ✓ You may find it impractical to apply much of the advice you read on team building, particularly if it is based on academic studies or the work of management consultancies.
- ✓ There will be certain factors in any team management situation where you have little or no control. These may include: team membership, team rewards, and individual rewards.
- ✓ The principles of team building offer a basis for your understanding but offer little in terms of practical day-to-day advice and assistance.

✓ Team-building principles are guidelines that you need to modify to suit your organization and team composition.

✓ Focus your time on managing the aspects of teambuilding you can affect and work within the constraints you have to accept.

✓ Ensure your team knows how success is going to be measured.

✓ Your team members will reflect your own behaviours.

✓ Demonstrate that you value all contributions made by team members.

✓ Ensure that you recognize and reward group success as well as that of the individual member.

Beware of `Teams in name only'

Some organizations use the word `team' as a collective noun to refer to any group of workers that perform a similar task.

For example, an organization may refer to the `Accounts Receivable Team,' to mean those people in the accounts department who chase late payments. In this case, these people all perform a similar role but they do not interact with each other very much and their work is done quite independently. Each `team member' has a list of customer invoices that have not been paid and that they are expected to chase payment for.

When a group of workers are performing this type of work but the organization still insists on referring to them collectively as a team, you should consider them to be a `team in name only' as opposed to a real team.

In this context a real team is a group of people who are working together synergistically to achieve something. This type of working is typified by project teams in which individuals who have complementary skills work together to achieve something that none of them could do individually.

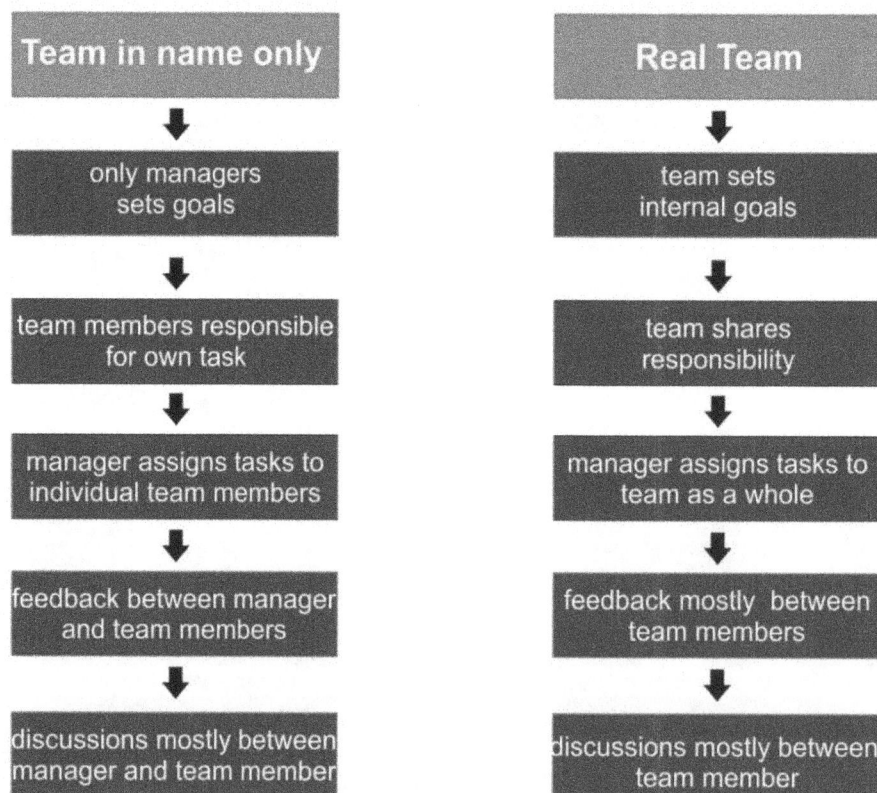

Team in name only	Real Team
⬇	⬇
only managers sets goals	team sets internal goals
⬇	⬇
team members responsible for own task	team shares responsibility
⬇	⬇
manager assigns tasks to individual team members	manager assigns tasks to team as a whole
⬇	⬇
feedback between manager and team members	feedback mostly between team members
⬇	⬇
discussions mostly between manager and team member	discussions mostly between team member

These differences are also evident when you look at the responsibilities of individual team members. For those in the Accounts Receivable Team each person is responsible only for their own individual tasks. Project team members, on the other hand, are accountable to each other for getting their own particular deliverables completed.

There is also a marked difference in the occurrence of conflict within these two teams. In the Accounts Receivable Team, conflict is rare because team members work independently. In contrast, the project team experiences a lot of internal disagreement about the best way to tackle certain parts of the project. This conflict is viewed as normal and understandable due to the nature of the work and interactions between the team members.

There are other types of team that could be placed somewhere in between `teams in name only' and real teams like a project team. You can save yourself a lot of frustration by recognizing that the closer a team is to being a `team in name only,' the less scope there is to apply team-building principles.

Key Points

- ✓ The structure of your team and the ethos of your organization will enable you to decide to what extent you are managing a real team or one in name only.

Team examples

The rest of this Book will use three real-life example teams to illustrate how teambuilding principles can be applied.

Each of these teams is quite different in its purpose and structure. These same team examples have been used in our `Team Leadership Styles' Book part of Management Sage Series . If you have already read that book and are familiar with these teams then you can go straight to the `Challenges you are most likely to encounter' section of each team example.

The example teams are:

- ✓ The Development Team
- ✓ The Customer Support Team
- ✓ The Steering Team

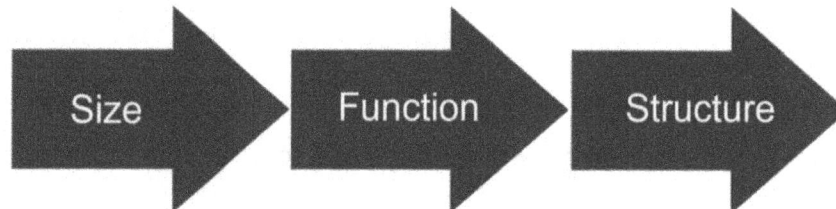

Size → Function → Structure

All of these example teams have a different size, function, and structure. They are based on real-life teams and are described in detail so that you can appreciate the differences between them and how these affect the way they are managed.

Background Information

These teams work within a large public utility company that was originally set up to provide water services. The company was originally owned by the state but has been privatized and now operates as a commercial organization.

The Water Services Regulator is responsible for ensuring that it continues to provide a quality service to all its customers and offers `value for money.' This body ensures also that the water company adheres to all the required legislative regulations.

In the past, the company has operated with a traditional authoritarian management style, but it is endeavoring to alter this to a more commercial and empowered style of management through its change management program. All managers are expected to develop, coach, and mentor their staff so that they adopt the competencies required by the new commercial organization.

Development Team Example

The IT department is headed up by a new director who has been brought in from a software company to update the organization's IT systems so that operations become more efficient and profitable.

Project Leader

In this scenario, you have been with the organization for five years and witnessed its evolution from a traditional water authority to a modern water company. You are currently a team leader and have just been given the responsibility of managing a key IT project for the next twelve months. You are responsible for ensuring that the project is delivered on time and within budget.

Project Objective

Your objective is to develop a suite of software programs to enable the company to monitor water quality throughout its catchment area. This will be a web-based IT system that allows water quality data collected from remote locations to be entered into a central database where it can be analyzed by the water quality department.

Composition of Team

The members of this team are all university graduates, their ages vary between 25 and 45 years, and they are all consider themselves relatively well paid. Five of the team members work directly for the company and three are freelance contractors.

Expert Users
seconded to
team (2)

Analyst
IT Dept (2)

Employees

Project
Leader

DBA IT dept
part-time (1)

Contractors

Programmers
(3)

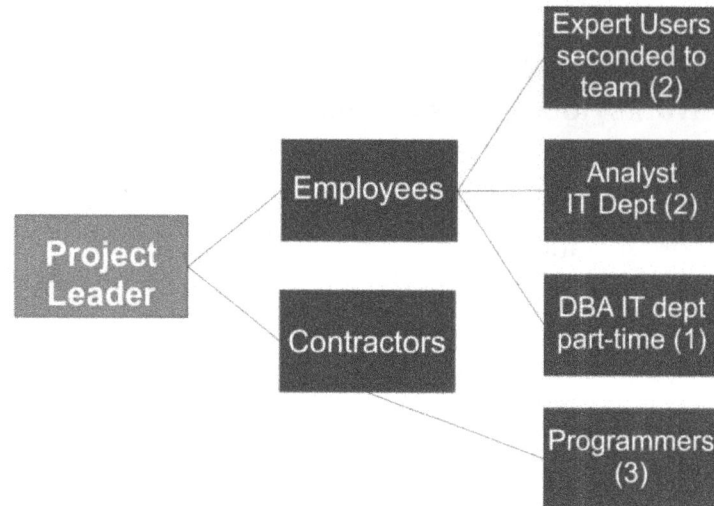

As you can see from the organizational chart above:

- The team has eight members excluding yourself
- Five of them are company employees
- Two have been seconded to the project from the water quality department
- One member, the database analyst, is only available to the team on a part-time basis
- Three of the team are external contractors

The first thing to notice about this particular team is that it is operating under what is known as a Matrix Management Environment. The expert users belong to the water quality department and the analysts and the DBA belong to the IT department. They are only assigned to you for the duration of the project, and when it is completed they will return to their respective departments. You do not have any direct control over them outside of the day-to-day running of the project. They still report to their own line managers, who are responsible for their appraisals, remuneration, promotions, etc.

The freelance contractors are all independent workers who have contracts with the company for the expected duration of the project. They have all worked for the company on previous projects and are keen to add another successful project to their resumes.

Challenges you are most likely to encounter

The composition of this development team highlights certain issues you could face as a project manager of this team. The high-level challenges are evident when you apply each of the principles of team building to this scenario.

Define Success Criteria

Arguably, the success criteria have already been defined as:
> *To develop web-based software that enables the company to centrally monitor water quality throughout its catchment area within twelve months.*

However, this is not terribly useful when managing the team on a day-to-day basis, which is why your first major task as project manager is to oversee the production of a detailed project plan that will specify all of the deliverables required and the timescales for producing them. A detailed description of these project milestones and individual work plans is beyond the scope of this eBook, but the important thing to note is that they define the most useful success criteria for individual team members as well as the project as a whole.

Lead by Example

It would quite common in this type of project team to find that the technical expertise of the IT staff and the contractors far outweighs your own. In addition, the expert users who have been seconded from the water quality department will know far more about this aspect of the business than you do.

This means that you cannot rely on your technical expertise to make you the natural leader. You will have to demonstrate your leadership through your organizational, planning, monitoring, and communications skills. You will also have to make your own assessment on how `knowledgeable' you consider each of these experts to be and adapt your management style to suit your findings. The rest of the team will be looking to you for direction and qualification of their actions.

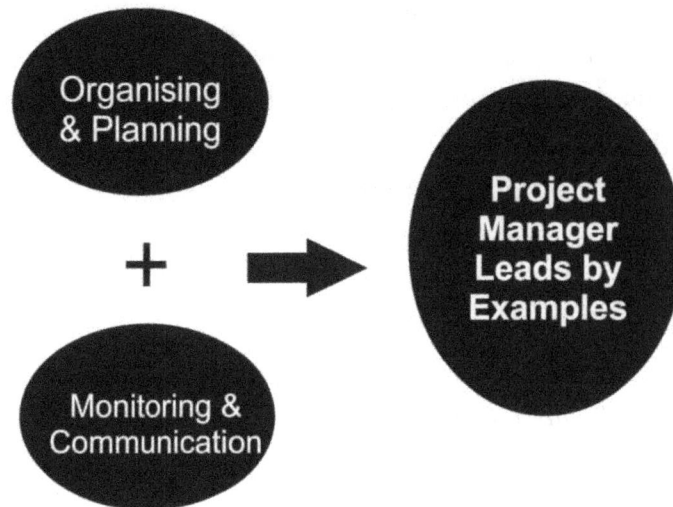

You will need to work with this team to set clearly defined tasks with an associated deadline and then allow them to use their expertise to deliver the required outputs. This would be done according to the project management methodology being used for this project. If you would like to improve your project management skills then you can refer our series of project management Books from Management Sage

You should be prepared to be flexible in the level of supervision and monitoring you allocate for each team member, depending on how they perform against the project plan over the first few weeks. This aspect of team leadership is dealt with in the eBook `Team Leadership Styles' which is also available from Management Sage

One of the most influential aspects of your leadership will be your communications and interpersonal skills, which will be visible to the team during team meetings. For example, do you make all members attend every meeting regardless of whether they have a contribution to make, or do you use other means of communication (e.g. emails) to keep the whole team informed?

Value All Contributions

You have direct control over how well each individual feels his or her contribution is received and valued by both yourself and the rest of the project team. You will be able to demonstrate this in your behaviour and readiness to consider and evaluate each contribution in terms of its input and worth to the project.

The difficulty here is in striking a balance between considering everyone's point of view and making efficient progress. Success in this area is a matter of chairing the team meetings effectively. This topic is dealt with in detail in the eBook `Meeting Skills--Acting as Chair' which is available from Management Sage.

Team Recognition and Reward

You have two sets of people within this project team and each set is rewarded in different ways. For the company employees, rewards will be tied up with their own individual appraisals and these remain the responsibility of their respective line managers.

You should make every effort to brief the relevant line managers regularly about the progress of the project and their own staff member's contribution to it. This is important for two reasons.

Firstly, if the project looks like it is going to overrun then the line managers need to know as soon as possible so that they do not commit the staff member to another project when you need them most. Asking a line manager if you can hang on to one of their staff who they have already scheduled other work for will only lead to conflict and you may end up losing a vital team member at the worst possible time.

Secondly, the line manager is still responsible for the staff member's annual appraisal and they will actively welcome your detailed input to this process when they are not in a position get the information themselves.

You may want to discuss with all employees how each person's individual objectives can be met through their project involvement and ensure your feedback to their line manager achieves this. For example, permanent members of staff can be motivated to act `beyond the call of duty' if they are told that this will be recognized in their annual appraisals or will count towards promotion.

In this way, you will be able to influence the recognition that each team member receives. You should also make sure that your written and verbal communications within the project team itself and to the senior management give recognition of each team member's performance and contribution whenever this is appropriate.

As discussed earlier, the freelance contractors are likely to place a high value on continuity of employment and would consider being recommended for other projects within your organization as a reward. If the organization is using the same contractors on an ongoing basis then offering them training opportunities can also work well for both parties. An extra place on an in-house training course costs very little, and provided that the
training increases the contractor's marketability it can be seen as a substantial reward.

Other Issues

Managing the DBA will be one of your biggest challenges in this project due to the fact that you only have part of their time. Meeting with them and asking the best way to keep them informed of progress and what sort of notice periods they require will gain their respect and commitment to your project. It also enables you to assess them as an individual, so that you can determine how much `management' they will require. Demonstrating to them that you are sensitive to their responsibilities outside of your project will go a long way to gaining their respect and commitment.

Most contractors are self-motivated professionals and will work best when given clear direction and support to allow them to do their job. Familiarize yourself with their contract terms so that you avoid any potential areas of conflict. For example:

- What will happen if they need to work more hours than the contracts stipulate in order to complete the project on time?
- Are they entitled to take any personal holiday time during the duration of the project?
- If they have a serious illness can you terminate the contract and get a replacement?

Getting as many senior people as possible on your side is vital because you will continually be competing for resources in this matrix management environment. Discovering which senior executives are champions of the web-based systems and their reasons why will help you overcome any resource problems you may face.

Furnished with this knowledge you will understand whom you need to keep informed of progress and any potential problems, as well as the best ways to communicate with these stakeholders. For example:

- Online water quality data will become a legal requirement in eighteen months. This means that the Finance Director has an interest in the project because of heavy fines if this requirement is not met.
- 40% of customers are in remote areas where the water quality is highly variable. This means that the Customer Services Director has an interest because of the ongoing impact on the business.
- Collection of water quality data is ad hoc and no formal standards exist. This means that the Operations Director has an interest because of the practical issues of collating this data at reduced cost.

Their view of you as a leader will also be influenced by how quickly you are able to overcome obstacles to progress.

Your experts from the water department, whilst they are responsible to you on a day-to-day basis, may still feel part of the water department, and as such may have conflicts of interests throughout the duration of the project. At the commencement of the project you will need to ensure that they feel their expertise is valued and can make a real contribution to the design of the system. You should take the time to understand the issues associated with these remote areas and what information is needed to properly assess the water quality.

It often helps to establish a rapport with such experts by asking them how aspects of data collection could change in the future especially with regard to legislation. This will enable the system to be designed with an element of adaptability built into it so that the organization can more easily respond to future needs.

In a team like this one where some individuals have much greater technical knowledge than others, you will need to encourage them to communicate in everyday language whenever possible. Some technical terms can't be avoided, but project members must be prepared to explain terms to others in the team as needed.

Your own behaviour in offering explanations for IT and industry terms will encourage an exchange of terminology as the analysts work with the expert users to define and design the system. It is important that you encourage the analysts to be honest in their definitions of how well the system can meet users' needs, as compromises from the business and IT aspects may be required in order to write the system specification.

Key Points

- The project manager is not an expert in all of the technical aspects of the project (database design, interface design, programming, and testing) but is still expected to coordinate the team's efforts.
- You are expected to ensure that the expensive human resources are utilized as effectively as possible and to produce a final deliverable within the allocated time and budget.
- Utilize the principles of team building as appropriate for the matrix management environment.
- Be aware of areas where a conflict of issue can arise within the team, e.g. seconded and part-time members.

Customer Support Team Example

Customer Support is one area of the Customer Services department, which is managed by the Customer Services Director who has been with the organization for over twenty years. His role has two main objectives relating to customer service:

1. To ensure customer complaints are resolved quickly and to both parties' satisfaction.
2. To ensure the number of complaints referred to the regulator are minimized.

Customer Support Manager

In this scenario, you have been working in the customer support area for three years and have recently been promoted to Customer Support Manager. You are responsible for ensuring that:

- Calls received by the support desk wait no longer than five minutes to be answered.
- 90% of issues are resolved on the first call.

Composition of Team

Your team is a group of 22 permanent members of staff who all report to you. The age of your team ranges from 16 to 28 years, with 18 of the staff being under 24 years. Ten members of the team are graduates and only seven members of the team have been with the organization for six months or more.

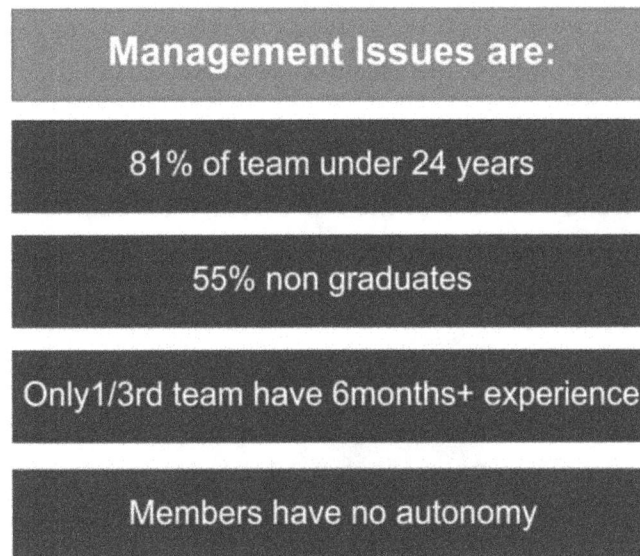

Management Issues are:

81% of team under 24 years

55% non graduates

Only 1/3rd team have 6months+ experience

Members have no autonomy

The team members have virtually no autonomy over their work because their workflow is handled by an automated telephone system, which routes queued calls to the first available team member.

The average time it takes to deal with a call is ten minutes and the average number of incoming calls per day is one thousand, which means that the team needs around 20 members to handle demand.

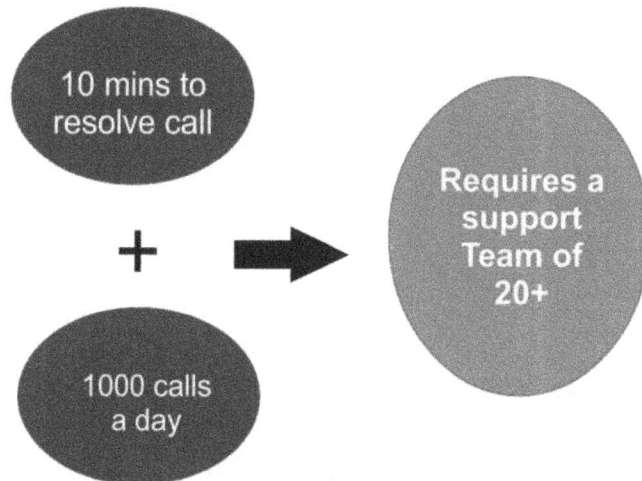

This explains why your team is large, much larger than the ideal of six people. You could look at splitting the team into two groups of eleven. This could be done through specialization--for example, billing queries and payment problems.

This type of split might be relatively easy to implement using the existing call handling system as customers already pre-select the reason for their call before getting through to the support desk. Splitting the group into two teams would also enable you to offer more focused training to each team.

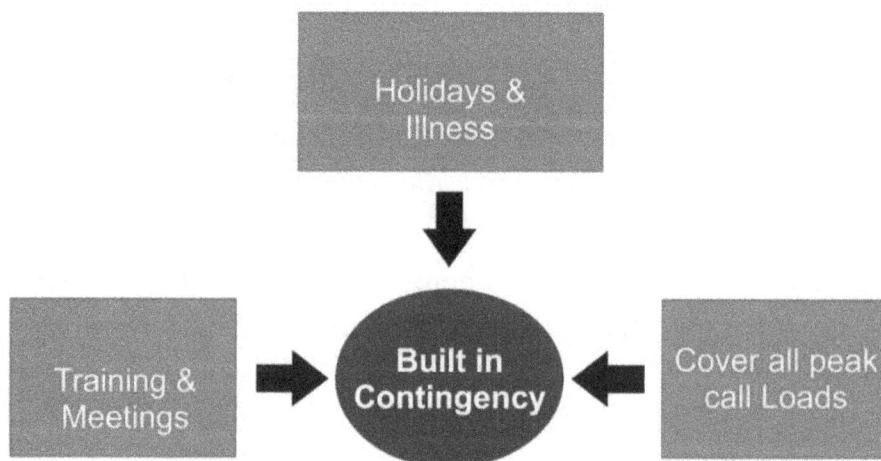

You would have to give careful consideration to how this would impact on your management time, as you would need to duplicate certain activities like team meetings.

Creating smaller groups within your team could also reduce areas of conflict that you have identified within the team; for example some team members are prone to antagonize each other for `entertainment' in their otherwise mundane and repetitive day.

Challenges you are most likely to encounter

Unlike the development team, your team has not been selected on the basis of their individual skills. You have been given this team to manage and you will have to work with the team members you have and do your best to meet your objective.

Define Success Criteria

The success criteria for the customer support team are visible to the team as a `mission statement' pinned to the office notice board.

- Calls received by the support desk wait no longer than five minutes to be answered.
- 90% of issues to be resolved on the first call.

There are two problems with these criteria, which have been set by someone in the company who has no idea of the day-to-day workings of the team.

Firstly, at peak times, the number of incoming calls is such that even if all of them are dealt with as quickly as possible, some callers will still be waiting for more than five minutes before their call is answered. In fact it would be necessary to double the size of the team to achieve this target at peak times--something that is totally unrealistic.

Secondly, whilst over 95% of the billing queries are resolved on the first call, only 60% of the payment problems are. This is because the payment problems often require the team member to obtain information from banks and the state welfare department. When this happens, they agree to call the customer back later--something that the customers prefer, rather than being kept waiting. Since payment problems make up around 30% of the

incoming calls, this makes the 90% target impossible to achieve.

The implications of this for you as a manager are that the success criteria are inappropriate for your team and you need to take action on this straightaway. No one likes being set targets that are unrealistic or impossible and it is quite likely that the consistent failure to hit these targets is badly affecting team morale. This is something you will need to take up with your director, once you have developed some success criteria that would be motivational for your team as well as acceptable to him.

You could also try to boost motivation by having some `unofficial' success criteria of your own. For example, you could use the call statistics output by the call management system to post a league table showing the team performance every week. This would give the team some targets to beat (i.e. last week's figures) and allow you to give them some feedback about their performance that was both meaningful and fair.

Lead by Example

Your first challenge as team leader is to change the perceptions of any of your team members who you have previously worked alongside on the customer support desk from seeing you as a co-worker to seeing you as a manager. You need to demonstrate the competencies of a manager through your behaviors. For example, coach and mentor team members how best to deal with difficult calls instead of taking over the call and resolving the problem for them.

From your knowledge of working on the support desk you will be able to empathize with your team. Your three years of industry knowledge will benefit the team considerably as two-thirds of your team will have less than six months' experience.

Whilst your team has no autonomy over their work, as their manager you can help them to feel they have some control by letting the team members organize lunch and break covers themselves. You will need to set the parameters they must adhere to--for example, at least twelve members must be available to answer calls between 12pm and 2pm.

Value all Contributions

You need to demonstrate that you welcome their feedback from customer calls. Very often, the first sign that the organization has done something to confuse or annoy customers is an increase in the frequency of incoming customer calls.

For example, the new design of bill may be misleading, or it is unclear to the customer what action to take if they have problems paying. Both of these issues would result in the support desk receiving additional calls. Being sensitive to any changes in the nature or frequency of customer problems would be an important part of your job. In this scenario, feeding back this type of information to the relevant manager or director so that
the company can reword the information and the bills would represent an improvement in customer service and also reduce the number of incoming calls that your team needs to deal with.

Often issues raised will not be so easily solved, but if you show that you are fair and consistent in your dealings with your staff they will feel valued and more willing to express their views when asked.

Team Recognition and Reward

In this type of team your most difficult task is to keep your team motivated and committed to the organization. The transient nature of the team is reflected in the high turnover of staff, with two-thirds of your team having been in the job for less than six months. It may also reflect the high levels of stress that the team members are under as they deal with irate and agitated customers all day.

You may decide to negotiate with your director to split the annual bonus for your team over the four quarters so that the team get more regular incentives, rewards, and recognition. If this is not a possibility then you may want to discuss other ways to recognize your team's achievements--for example through meal vouchers, theater or club tickets, go-karting or paintball vouchers, etc.

Recognition can also be given for highlighting a certain type of call that requires specialist resources to resolve. An example could be bringing to your attention the rising number of calls due to communication problems, e.g. callers needing special assistance, elderly or those who speak little English.

As manager you will have access to numerous statistics, which will highlight to you any team member who is having problems with high absenteeism or lack of motivation. It is important that you have regular contact with each member so that you can discuss such issues, understand the reasons behind them, and seek a resolution.

One of your greatest challenges as a manager of this type of team will be your ability to motivate and reward the individual team members sufficiently to retain them. You will need to look at ways to counter the lack of career opportunities, perceived low pay, and the endless stream of difficult calls.

Looking at all the ways your organization allows you to reward your staff will help to a degree, but it is likely you will need to be creative in offering non-financial rewards. You could allow a dress-down or theme dressing day to raise money for charity. In fact, anything that would improve team spirit whilst maintaining a high level of customer service. For the individual you may be able to gain tickets to a corporate sponsored event, e.g. a sporting or cultural event.

Key Points

- As Customer Support Manager you will have little flexibility or choice over who is in your team, but you can organize the individuals you have in the way that best achieves your objectives. It is important to:
- Exhibit your own personal commitment to your work and actively listen to team members' comments and feedback to gauge the mood of the team.
- Look at ways to ensure sub-groups within your large team are operating as close to the ideal group size as practical.
- Utilize your organization's reward structure and source creative ways to offer additional team and individual incentives, e.g. tickets to corporate sponsored events
- Use formal and informal means of communication to identify, defuse, and address issues of motivation or conflict.
- Create a thorough induction pack to handle staff turnover issues and bring new team members up to speed quickly.

Steering Team Example

Many corporations make use of Steering Teams in their drive to stay ahead of competitors, research future market trends, and plan for changes in legislation that will affect them. Organizations that operate in highly regulated sectors also use this type of team to consider the impact of new rulings on the business.

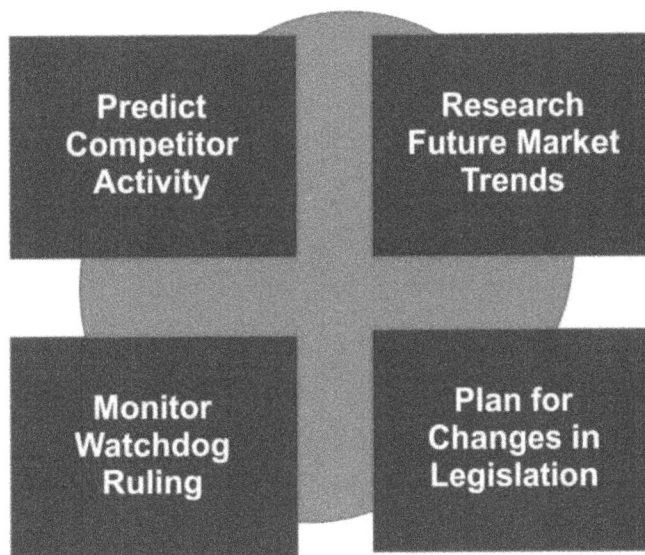

Steering Team Leader

In this scenario, you are the Business Development Executive of the water company. You have been an employee for two years. Your previous experience includes commercial legal expertise and management of deregulation in the leading telecommunications corporation. Your team's longterm objective is to identify the most profitable business opportunities that are available to the water company following the deregulation of their operations. The legislation removes the restrictions that previously meant that the organization could only sell water services.

The team also has a short-term objective to present a report on the potential opportunity and profitability of selling insurance to the water company's existing customer base of 14 million households.

Composition of Team

The Steering Team has some permanent members and some who have been brought in to look at specific issues. The permanent membership is made up of a senior person from each department within the company and the function of this group is to identify new business opportunities as described earlier.

In order to evaluate an opportunity, the team leader will need to bring in additional expertise from both inside and outside of the company.

For example, when investigating the possibility of selling insurance to its customer base the Steering Team would need to bring in representatives of:

- Customer Services Department
- IT Department
- Finance Department
- Regional Directors
- Marketing Department
- Law Firm
- Potential Partner Insurance Company
- Insurance Industry Regulator

This is a total of seventeen people as shown in the diagram below.

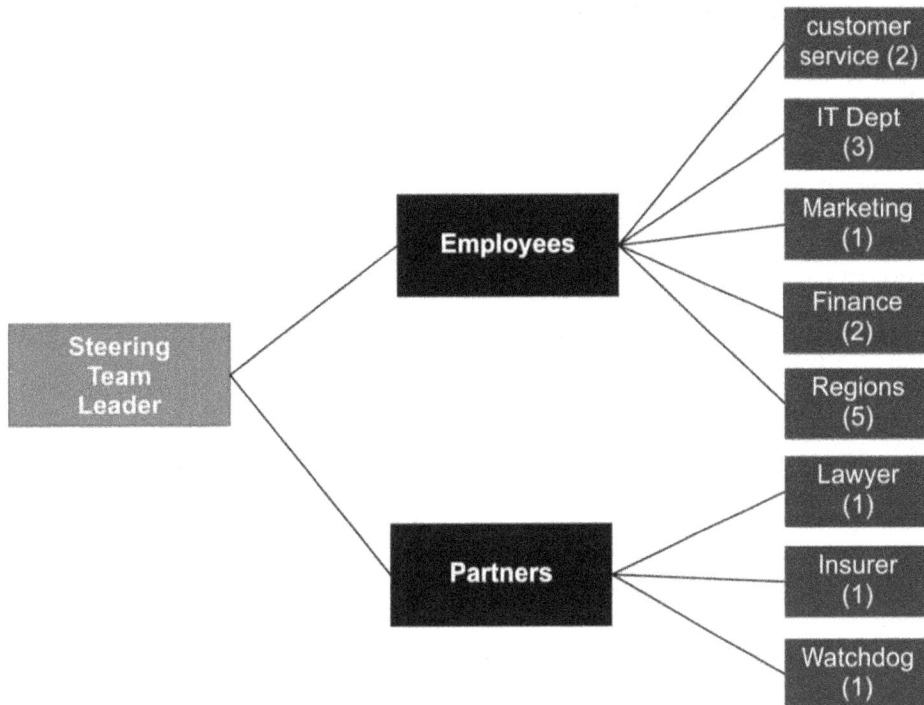

Each team member has his or her own responsibilities and career path, and even the permanent members of the team are only assigned to it on a part-time basis. Your team size of seventeen people is on the large side, but it is necessary to have all the departments and partners represented who could be impacted by the decision to sell insurance. An informed decision simply cannot be made without involving all of these parties.

Challenges you are most likely to encounter

As team leader of the Steering Team your main challenge is to strike a balance between keeping the team focused on specific projects (in this case the decision to move into the insurance market) and allowing the team the freedom to explore other possible areas of interest to the business.

Define Success Criteria

The success criteria for this team are more difficult to specify than for the other examples we have looked at. Whilst the current project provides this team with a short-term goal, the output from this project needs to be properly defined and a deadline set. If this is not done, then it will be difficult to motivate the team members, who still have their normal day-to-day responsibilities, to allocate the necessary time and effort.

At the same time, the permanent members of the team need to be thinking strategically about the changing business environment, which will be continuously presenting new opportunities for the company.

These two distinct areas will need to be managed separately to prevent the team from either becoming totally focused on the current project or alternatively spending too much time on strategic issues at the expense of the current project.

With this in mind, the best approach would be to keep these two functions separate.

All meetings and communication relating to the insurance project should be limited to that topic alone. This policy will need to be strictly enforced because there is always a tendency for this type of team to become a general talking shop and whilst some viable ideas may occasionally emerge it is an inefficient use of everyone's time.

There should be a formal procedure for bringing new opportunities to the attention of the team. This could involve a team member preparing a report that is then considered by a sub-group before being presented at a monthly strategy meeting at which individual projects are not discussed.

As leader of this team your responsibility is to concentrate all the efforts of the members on the current issue, whether it is an ongoing project or consideration of a new opportunity. This will involve setting meeting agendas that are highly focused, as well as making sure that the agenda is stuck to.

Lead by Example

Your own expertise and knowledge is well known within the group, but each individual is involved in your team because of the knowledge they can contribute, so you need to work towards gaining from them. Your own behavior will define and portray your expectations of others:

- Always arrive on time
- Prepare fully for each meeting
- Complete all your actions in a timely fashion
- Always issue accurate meeting minutes swiftly after each session
- Communicate clearly
- Ensure your commitment to the objective is evident in all your judgments

You will find that your role is comparable to that of a meeting `Chair' where you have to listen to information being communicated and make a decision about what actions need to be taken. This decision needs to have the support of the team and should be arrived at through discussion and consensus.

One problem that you could come across in this scenario is that you will often be trying to control a meeting in which most of the attendees have as much or more seniority than you do. This can be made easier if the format of the meetings is as formal as you can make it and includes timed slots for each agenda item. How to stay in control of meetings where you do not have seniority is dealt with in detail in the Book `Meeting Skills--Acting as Chair,' which is available in Management Sage Series.

Another key activity for you as leader of the Steering Team is to develop the support of the senior management for the team's investigation and ultimately their decision on its objective.

Value all Contributions

Wherever possible you should break up the team into sub-teams because most discussions will only impact on certain areas of the business and simply do not need everyone's involvement. This will not only save the company money but will minimize any resentment that team members feel as a result of being distracted from their other work.

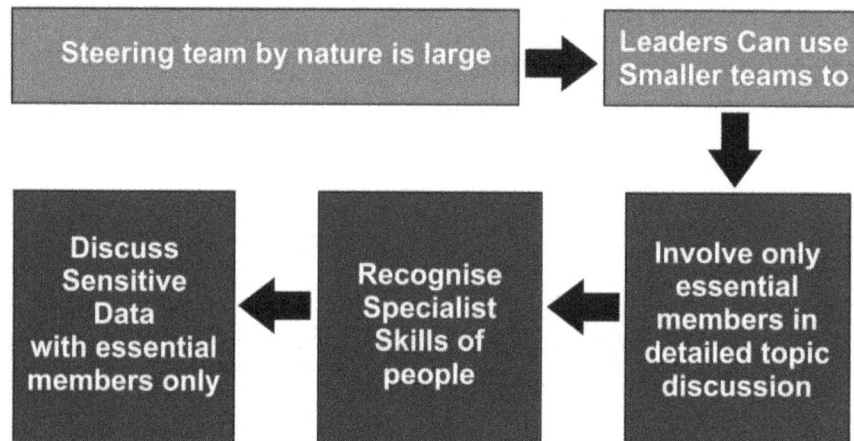

```
┌─────────────────────────────────────┐    ┌──────────────────┐
│ Steering team by nature is large     │ ─► │ Leaders Can use   │
└─────────────────────────────────────┘    │ Smaller teams to  │
                                            └──────────────────┘
                                                     │
                                                     ▼
┌──────────────┐   ┌──────────────┐   ┌──────────────────┐
│ Discuss      │   │ Recognise    │   │ Involve only     │
│ Sensitive    │ ◄─│ Specialist   │ ◄─│ essential        │
│ Data         │   │ Skills of    │   │ members in       │
│ with essential│  │ people       │   │ detailed topic   │
│ members only │   │              │   │ discussion       │
└──────────────┘   └──────────────┘   └──────────────────┘
```

Only very rarely will you need to call the whole Steering Team together and you can use a variety of communications methods--email, secure intranet, and meeting minutes--to keep everyone informed of each sub-group's progress and findings.

Whenever you have sub-groups working in this way, you will need to make sure that the whole team, and not just the sub-group, knows the contribution of each team member. Many of the members of this team are motivated by the career-boosting visibility and recognition that team membership brings. Since you are not in a position to offer monetary rewards, you need to make sure that everyone feels as though their efforts are recognized as widely as possible within the company.

You can do this by communicating your appreciation for their input or the role they have played; it may be something as simple as saying `Thank you' to the individual and in team situations. Listing all contributions in meeting minutes and making sure that any report summaries you send give full credit to the authors can also help achieve this.

Team Recognition and Reward

Involvement in this team is welcomed because each individual appreciates the benefit their inclusion provides for their career development.

The reward people are looking for in this type of team is career-boosting recognition. As team leader, your objective is to make sure that each participant feels that senior management will recognize his or her contribution as discussed earlier.

This doesn't mean that you don't need to bother showing your appreciation and acknowledging individuals' contributions. In fact, it is essential that you as leader of the team do recognize the role each individual has played at each stage of the investigation and the decision-making process.

Without this recognition from you, some team members may feel undervalued, and this could result in resentment and a lack of motivation. It is important that this recognition occurs within the Steering Team, at a senior level within the organization, and as appropriate within any partner organizations.

Key Points

- The Steering Team is a unique team that is composed to find individuals who each have complementary skills and knowledge. In this instance the team leader devolves responsibility as much as possible, offering recognition and reward to team members
- Using careful questioning to tease out key facts demonstrates your appreciation of an individual's contribution.
- Lead the team by exhibiting the behaviours you expect and desire others to display and adopt.
- As manager of the Steering Team you are responsible for managing the public relations issues of the project within the organization.
- Clearly communicate your appreciation and thanks for each member's input so that everyone receives the recognition and reward they desire.
- Steering Teams may be quite large, with many being between 12 and 25 people. You can easily divide such a team into smaller sub-groups of working parties focusing on specific aspects.

Summary

Successful team building in the workplace has more to do with applying some key principles to the team you have been given, rather than recruiting `perfect' team members in order to build an ideal team from scratch.

The four key principles of team building are:

Define Success Criteria

This means defining and communicating the team objective so that it is easily understood by everyone and allows all team members to contribute, regardless of their skills and experience.

Lead by Example

Leading by example means exhibiting the same professional behaviors to everyone you interact with, whether they are inside or outside your team. This includes customers and suppliers as well as other people within your organization.

Value All Contributions

You will need to show that you value each member of the team and that their views matter to you regardless of the role they play. One simple way to exhibit this is by ensuring all views are heard when talking about issues at a team meeting or discussion.

Reward Success

You will usually have the ability to reward those team members you are directly responsible for. However, the extent to which you are able to offer truly motivating rewards, especially monetary, will be influenced by your organization's culture and the amount of decision-making power you have.

There will always be certain factors in any team management situation where you have little or no control. These may include: team membership, team rewards, and individual rewards.

The principles of team building offer a basis for your understanding but you will need to modify them to suit your organization and team composition. Remember, focus your time on managing the aspects of team building you can affect and work within the constraints you have to accept.

Preface

This eBook has been written for managers who find themselves in a team leadership role. It uses three real-life examples to illustrate how different leadership styles can be applied to suit different types of team.

You will learn:

- Where transactional leadership will be appropriate and where it is counter-productive to the team's objective.
- How transformational leadership can enhance motivation, morale, and performance by creating a sense collective identity.
- The four key elements of transformational leadership and how to apply them in
- your interactions with your team.
- How situational leadership can be used to alter your leadership style to suit the
- ability and motivation of your team to.
- How to give your team sufficient freedom to maximize their personal development and job satisfaction, while still achieving their targets.

Introduction

Probably the most important part of becoming any sort of leader in the modern work-place is to be the person that others choose to follow. Even where compulsion is possible, it tends not to work very well.

If people decide that they don't want to do things your way, then they can find any number of ingenious ways to undermine your wishes. Even if the obstructive behaviour justifies dismissal, firing someone always has negative consequences for morale, focus, and productivity.

In fact, you can end up spending so much time and effort defending your decision to your boss, co-workers, or an employment tribunal that you don't have any time left to do your job properly.

If you want to take a leadership role, then the most important questions you can ask are:

- Which leadership style is the most appropriate?
- Which leadership style is most prevalent in your organization?
- Why should my team follow my lead?
- How can I alter my competencies and behaviours to become this type of leader?

The answers to these questions depend on your role, your team, and the task at hand. Whilst there are some skills that you will need to develop in order to be an effective leader, your role, your team, and the task will all affect which of these skills you use.

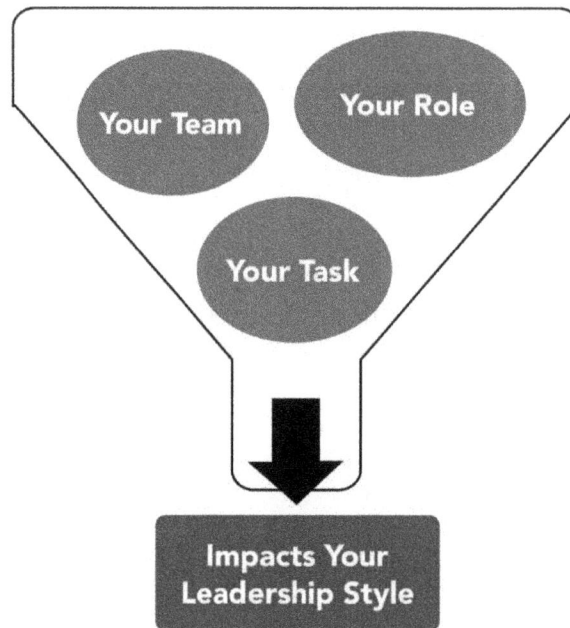

Before getting down to answering the question of why people would choose to follow your lead, you will need to understand the different styles of leadership available and the different types of team that are found in the workplace.

The fact that there are such a variety of possible types of team makes it impractical to generalize too much when discussing leadership styles. Throughout this eBook we will use three real-life examples of teams that are very different in their purpose and make-up.

Key Points

- Being the person that others choose to follow is the key to effective team leadership.
- The optimum leadership style will depend on your role, your team, and the task at hand.

Team examples

You should be aware from experience of the wide variety of teams that exist throughout modern organizations. The remainder of this eBook will use three real-life examples of teams to illustrate how different team leadership styles can be applied to suit different types of team.

These same team examples have been used in our 'Principles of Team Building' eBook. If you are familiar with each one's size, function, and structure you can go straight to the 'Leadership Theories' section.

The example teams are:

- The Development Team
- The Customer Support Team
- The Steering Team

Each of these teams is quite different in its purpose and structure, and has a different size, function, and composition. They will illustrate that there is no 'best way' to manage a team and that you will need to use your own judgment and understanding of your organization when considering 'best' how to manage your own team.

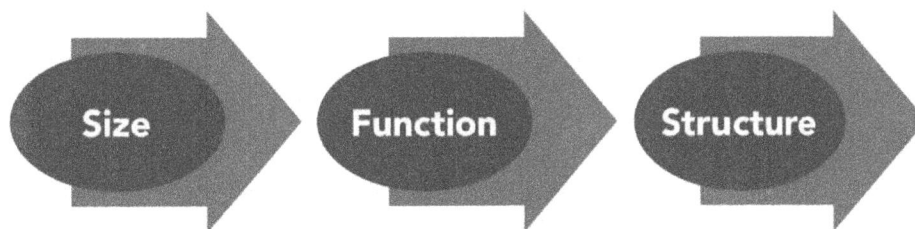

All of these example teams work within a public utility company, a Water Company. They are based on real-life teams and are described in detail so that you can appreciate the differences between them and how these affect the way they are managed.

Background Information

These teams work within a large public utility company that was originally set up to provide water services. The company was originally owned by the state but has been privatized and now operates as a commercial organization.

The Water Services Watchdog is responsible for ensuring that it continues to provide a quality service to all its customers and offers 'value for money.' This body ensures also that the water company adheres to all the required legislative regulations.

In the past, the company has operated with a traditional authoritarian management style, but it is endeavouring to alter this to a more commercial and empowered style of management through its change management program. All managers are expected to develop, coach, and mentor their staff so that they adopt the competencies required by the new commercial organization.

Each of these teams requires a different type of leadership to make it successful. How and which style is best for you to adopt is discussed in the section 'Leadership Theories.'

Development Team Example

The IT department is headed up by a new director who has been brought in from a software company to update the organization's IT systems so that operations become more efficient and profitable.

Project Leader

In this scenario, you have been with the organization for five years and witnessed its evolution from a traditional water authority to a modern water company. You are currently a team leader and have just been given the responsibility of managing a key IT project for the next twelve months. You are responsible for ensuring that the project is delivered on time and within budget.

Project Objective

Your objective is to develop a suite of software programs to enable the company to monitor water quality throughout its catchment area. This will be a web-based IT system that allows water quality data collected from remote locations to be entered into a central database where it can be analyzed by the water quality department.

Composition of Team

The members of this team are all university graduates, their ages vary between 25 and 45 years, and they are all consider themselves relatively well paid. Five of the team members work directly for the company and three are freelance contractors

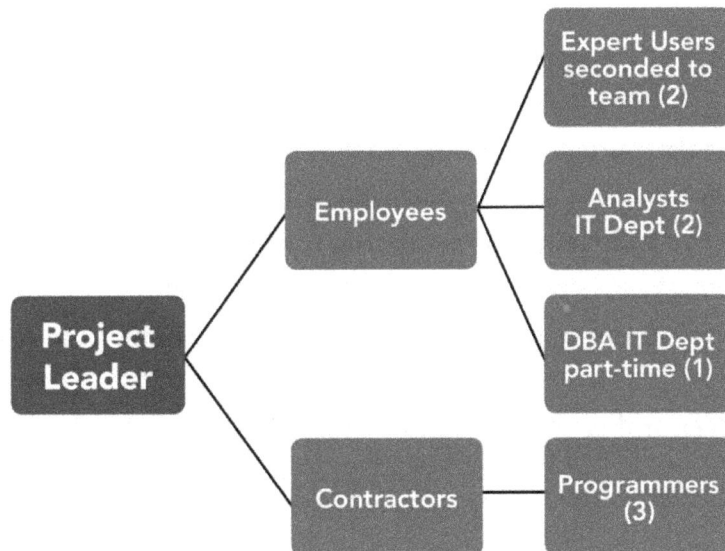

As you can see from the organizational chart above:

- The team has eight members excluding yourself
- Five of them are company employees
- Two have been seconded to the project from the water quality department
- One member, the database analyst, is only available to the team on a part-time basis
- Three of the team are external contractors

The first thing to notice about this particular team is that it is operating under what is known as a Matrix Management Environment. The expert users belong to the water quality department and the analysts and the DBA belong to the IT department. They are only assigned to you for the duration of the project, and when it is completed they will return to their respective departments. You do not have any direct control over them out- side of the day-to-day running of the project. They still report to their own line managers, who are responsible for their appraisals, remuneration, promotions, etc.

The freelance contractors are all independent workers who have contracts with the company for the expected duration of the project. They have all worked for the company on previous projects and are keen to add another successful project to their resumes.

Customer Support Team Example

Customer Support is one area of the Customer Services department, which is managed by the Customer Services Director who has been with the organization for over twenty years. His role has two main objectives relating to customer service:

- To ensure customer complaints are resolved quickly and to both parties' satisfaction.
- To ensure the number of complaints referred to the watchdog are minimized.

Customer Support Manager

In this scenario, you have been working in the customer support area for three years and have recently been promoted to Customer Support Manager. You are responsible for ensuring that:

- Calls received by the support desk wait no longer than five minutes to be answered.
- 90% of issues are resolved on the first call.

Composition of Team

Your team is a group of 22 permanent members of staff who all report to you. The age of your team ranges from 16 to 28 years, with 18 of the staff being under 24 years. Ten members of the team are graduates and only seven members of the team have been with the organization for six months or more.

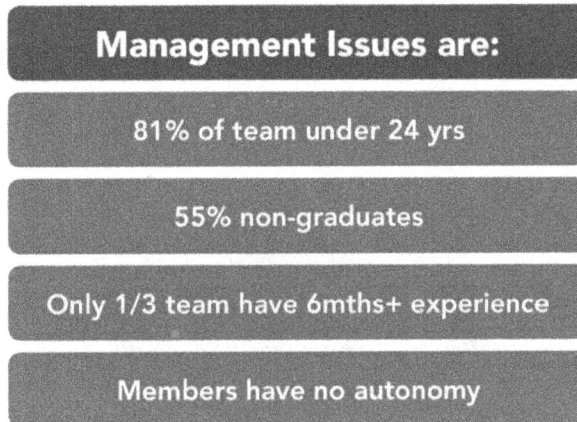

Management Issues are:

- 81% of team under 24 yrs
- 55% non-graduates
- Only 1/3 team have 6mths+ experience
- Members have no autonomy

The team members have virtually no autonomy over their work because their workflow is handled by an automated telephone system which routes queued calls to the first available team member.

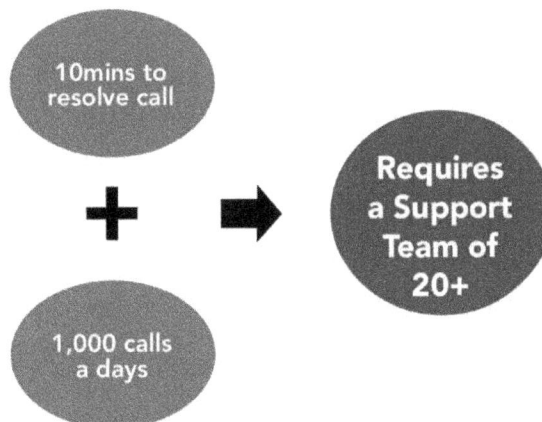

10mins to resolve call

+

1,000 calls a days

→ Requires a Support Team of 20+

The average time it takes to deal with a call is ten minutes and the average number of incoming calls per day is one thousand, which means that the team needs around 20 members to handle demand.

Steering Team Example

Many corporations make use of Steering Teams in their drive to stay ahead of competitors, research future market trends, and plan for changes in legislation that will affect them. Organizations that operate in highly regulated sectors also use this type of team to consider the impact of new rulings on the business.

Steering Team Leader

In this scenario, you are the Business Development Executive of the water company. You have been an employee for two years. Your previous experience includes commercial legal expertise and management of deregulation in the leading telecommunications corporation. Your team's long-term objective is to identify the most profitable business opportunities that are available to the water company following the deregulation of their operations. The legislation removes the restrictions that previously meant that the organization could only sell water services.

The team also has a short-term objective to present a report on the potential opportunity and profitability of selling insurance to the water company's existing customer base of 14 million households.

Composition of Team

The Steering Team has some permanent members and some who have been brought in to look at specific issues. The permanent membership is made up of a senior person from each department within the company and the function of this group is to identify new business opportunities as described earlier.

In order to evaluate an opportunity, the team leader will need to bring in additional expertise from both inside and outside of the company.

For example, when investigating the possibility of selling insurance to its customer base the Steering Team would need to bring in representatives of:

- Customer Services Department
- IT Department
- Finance Department
- Regional Directors
- Marketing Department
- Law Firm
- Potential Partner Insurance Company
- Insurance Watchdog

This is a total of seventeen people as shown in the diagram below

Each team member has his or her own responsibilities and career path, and even the permanent members of the team are only assigned to it on a part-time basis. Your team size of seventeen people is on the large side but it is necessary to have all the departments and partners represented who could be impacted by the decision to sell insurance. An informed decision simply cannot be made without involving all of these parties.

Leadership Theories

The subject of Leadership has been studied since antiquity. Literature on the topic reveals an evolving succession of theories. The earliest tend to focus on the character and personality of successful leaders, whilst later theories concentrate on what leaders actually do rather than on their innate qualities.

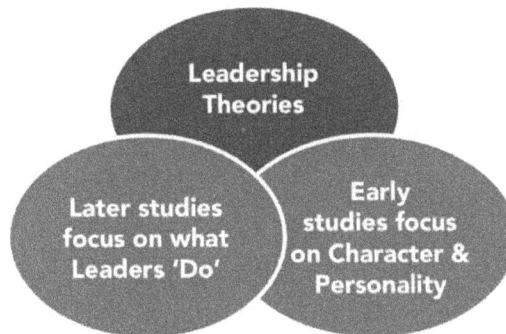

The earlier studies, which focused on the distinct qualities of how leaders behaved and the persona of individual leaders, are collectively known as 'Trait Theories.'

Early Trait Theories

These theories attempted to list the personal qualities associated with leadership and looked at the type of behaviours such individuals exhibited. Such studies saw these as the aspects that enabled leaders to influence others' behaviour and get them to help their leader achieve his or her goal.

From these studies can be discerned six basic qualities that describe the behavioural traits of leaders:

- Honesty and Integrity
- Emotional Maturity
- Motivation
- Self-confidence
- Cognitive Ability
- Achievement Drive

1. **Honesty and integrity**—words such as 'trustworthy,' 'reliable,' and 'open' would be used to describe the leader.
2. **Emotional maturity**—describes a person who is well adjusted and does not suffer from severe psychological disorders.
3. **Motivation**—can be described as an intense desire to lead others to reach shared goals.
4. **Self-confidence**—depicts someone who shows an unwavering belief in one's self, one's ideas, and one's ability.
5. **Cognitive ability**—portrays an individual that is capable of exercising good judgment, shows strong analytical abilities, and is conceptually skilled.
6. **Achievement drive**—refers to the high level of effort, ambition, energy, and initiative that leaders exhibit.

There is also a seventh quality, 'Other,' which pulls together certain traits that were felt not to fit into the six listed above. These are such things as charisma, creativity, and flexibility, which are often used when describing a respected leader.

'Other' traits: Charisma | Creativity | Flexibility

While it is true that some of the great political and military leaders of the past have shared these personal qualities, there are just as many exceptions. For example, three world-renowned military leaders of the Second World War illustrated a deficiency in at least one of the traits described above.

- **Winston Churchill**—the British wartime leader suffered from severe clinical depression.
- **Josef Stalin**—the Soviet leader could hardly be described as trustworthy, reliable, and open.
- **Adolf Hitler**—the German leader, among many other deficiencies, showed a lack of judgment when he went against the advice of almost all of his generals and chose to invade the Soviet Union, an act that was directly responsible for his ultimate defeat.

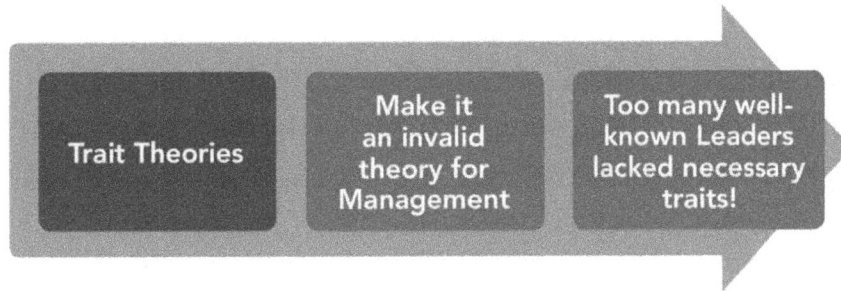

By simply selecting these three great leaders one can illustrate that trait theories do not stand up to scrutiny even in the context of political or military leadership, and are usually the product of wishful thinking and nationalistic hero worship.

Key Points

- Early leadership theories tend to focus on the character and personality of successful leaders, whilst later theories concentrate on what leaders actually do.
- Trait theories do not stand up to scrutiny even in the context of political or military leadership

Leadership for management

The need for effective leaders within organizations has led to theories and methodologies that rely on behaviours that can be learned rather than 'traits' that a person either does or does not have.

Managers are now expected to actively develop their leadership skills and to know how to adapt them to best accomplish the task at hand.

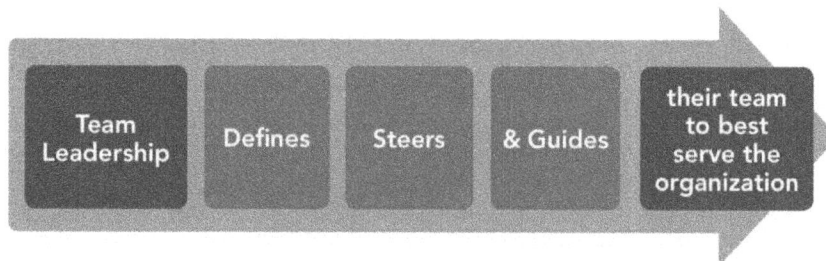

For the purpose of this eBook 'leadership' in the context of team building means defining, steering, and guiding your team members down the path that you believe will best serve the interests of the organization.

There are four practical leadership styles that you need to consider, whether you are a Customer Support Manager, Project Manager, or Steering Team Manager. You need to assess how adopting each style would benefit or hinder you in the role of team leader

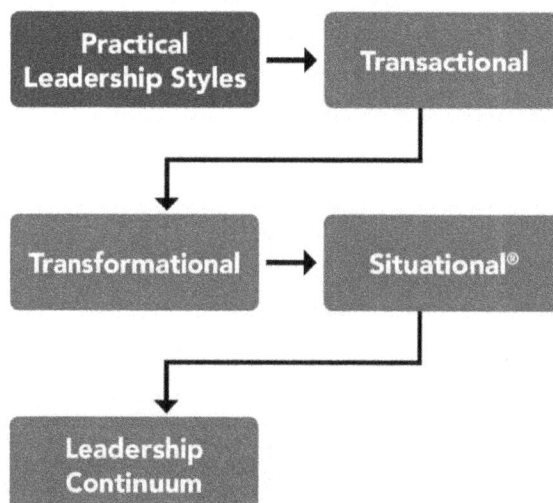

These practical leadership styles are:

- Transactional Leadership
- Transformational Leadership
- Situational Leadership
- The Leadership Continuum

The most important aspect of being a leader is deciding how much freedom to give your team. Too much, and they may not achieve their targets. Too little, and you will restrict their personal development and job satisfaction.

There is no easy answer to this problem and the best course of action is to consider each case on its merits with a clear appreciation of the risks involved of giving too much autonomy.

Key Points

- Managers are expected to actively develop their leadership skills and to know how to adapt them to best accomplish the task at hand.
- There are four practical leadership styles you should be aware of: Transactional Leadership, Transformational Leadership, Situational Leadership and The Leadership Continuum.

Transactional Leadership

The fundamental requirement for this style of leadership is that a 'transaction' exists between the leader and the team members. This transaction has two aspects:

- It involves the organization paying wages to team members in return for effort and compliance.
- The leader/manager has the right to discipline an employee if their work does not meet an appropriate standard.

The power of transactional leaders comes from their formal authority and level of responsibility within the organization. Such leaders are primarily concerned with establishing the criteria for rewarding team members for good performance. This is referred to as 'Contingent Reward,' e.g. praise. Team members are rewarded for their efforts—for example for completing set goals on time, or in recognition of handling a difficult situation well.

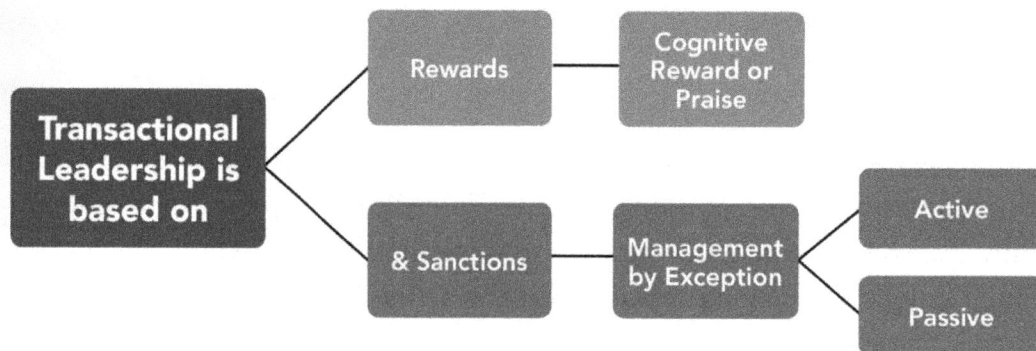

In situations where the team member's performance is below the acceptable standard, you will need to apply appropriate sanctions. This is known as 'Management by Exception.' This corrective action can either be active or passive. If you adopt an active sanction then you are continually monitoring the team member's performance and correcting any errors as they occur. Alternatively you can use a passive sanction where you wait for issues to come up before fixing the problems.

If you adopt this style of leadership then you will focus your activities on the processes of supervision, organization, and group performance. You will be concerned with efficiency rather than forward-thinking ideas. You will have to be comfortable with being authoritative and always telling your members what to do.

This type of leadership makes certain assumptions about your team. Firstly, that they are only motivated by reward or punishment; they have no selfmotivation. Secondly, that they know from the outset that they must obey your instructions without question and expect to be closely monitored and controlled.

Equipped with these facts you will be aware that this style of leadership is only appropriate in certain situations.

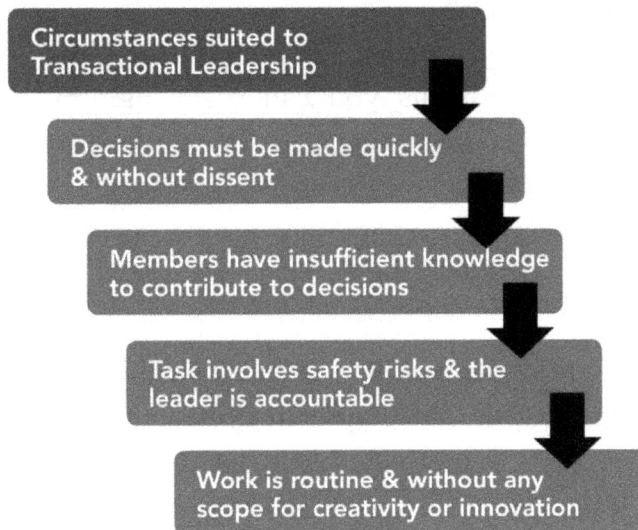

Circumstances suited to Transactional Leadership

Decisions must be made quickly & without dissent

Members have insufficient knowledge to contribute to decisions

Task involves safety risks & the leader is accountable

Work is routine & without any scope for creativity or innovation

The situations where transactional leadership is appropriate are where:

- Decisions must be made quickly and without dissent
- Subordinates do not have sufficient knowledge to contribute to decisions
- The work involves safety risks and the leader will be held accountable
- The work is routine and there is no scope for creativity or innovation

If you find yourself in such a situation then you may want to adopt this style of leadership.

Applied to the Team Examples

Looking at our three example teams you can easily ascertain where transactional leadership will be appropriate and where it is counter-productive to the team's objective.

Development Team

The nature of this team requires its members to use their own knowledge and skills to solve the issues raised during the development cycle of the new web-based systems. They are also by character self-motivated and are expected to and want to work independently of the team leader in how they deliver the tasks and goals they have been set by the project manager.

As project manager you also expect considerable input into discussions as part of the decision-making process from all team members, often seeking forward-thinking and innovative approaches to problems you come across during the development process.

These characteristics of the project team make it impossible for you as manager to adopt a transactional style leadership.

Customer Support Team

As Customer Support Manager you may find that many of the benefits of the Transactional Leadership style suit your team structure. The nature of the work is often repetitive and the vast majority of tasks require the members to follow a predefined path, which leaves little or no room for creativity and innovation.

Your main focus is to ensure that an acceptable level of service is maintained and you will be continually monitoring the call statistics. By its very nature of continual observation you are adopting 'active management by exception' in your approach to leadership.

Throughout the day you, as well as the team members, can see the total number of calls received and how well you are meeting your targets. The software enables you to closely monitor and control your team. It also reports on how well each member is executing their role, so you are quickly able to identify anyone who is underperforming and praise those who are working well.

Consistent underperformers usually leave the team of their own accord quite quickly, so sanctions do not often have to be instigated. This is because other team members will be constantly aware of a poor performer and may react negatively towards this person, as they have to work harder to compensate for a poor performer; if they don't, the whole team suffers. Motivation comes as a result of not wanting to let the team down rather than any personal sense of achievement.

This is one of the reasons why most call centres having a high rate of absenteeism and staff turnover. The latter also reflects the fact that the Customer Support Team is one of the few workgroups within the organization that will actually dismiss people during their probationary period if the team leader feels that they are not able to perform. It can also indicate that some people resent being treated in an autocratic way.

One reason for these problems in customer support teams arises from the stressful and unrewarding nature of the job. As manager you can try to counterbalance this by providing an opportunity for some autonomy by letting the members decide who works which shifts (within strict guidelines to maintain service quality) and who has what break and lunch times. This small freedom in an otherwise highly structured environment can do a lot to boost morale.

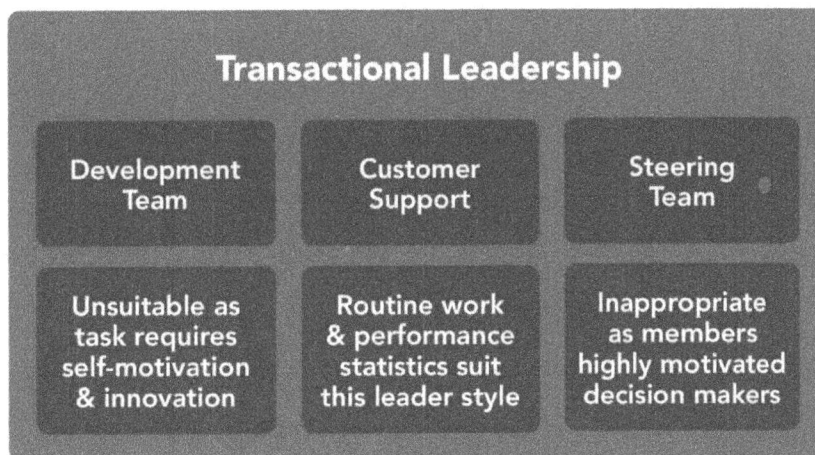

Transactional Leadership		
Development Team	Customer Support	Steering Team
Unsuitable as task requires self-motivation & innovation	Routine work & performance statistics suit this leader style	Inappropriate as members highly motivated decision makers

Steering Team

Since all members of the Steering Team have been selected for their ability to contribute their knowledge to benefit the investigation and the organization, they are by their very nature self-motivated and innovative thinkers and decision makers.

The responsive nature of the transactional leader is out of place in this type of team, and the team's very existence questions the current organizational composition through its need to think innovatively. In some instances as manager of the Steering Team you may need to use transactional leadership to impose a decision on a relatively minor issue to avoid wasting time trying to reach a consensus.

Key Points

- The power of transactional leaders comes from their formal authority and \level of responsibility within the organization.
- If you adopt this style of leadership then you will focus your activities on the processes of supervision, organization, and group performance.
- The situations where transactional leadership is appropriate are where: decisions must be made quickly and without dissent, subordinates do not have sufficient knowledge to contribute to decisions, the work involves safety risks and the leader will be held accountable or where the work is routine and there is no scope for creativity or innovation.

Transformational Leadership

Transformational leadership is based on the ability of the leader to motivate followers through their charisma, intellectual stimulation, and individual consideration. J.M. Burns first described it in the context of political leaders as a process in which 'leaders and followers help each other to advance to a higher level of morale and motivation.'

Burns showed that the leader encourages followers to come up with new and unique ways to challenge the status quo and to alter the environment to support being successful. Such leaders enhance motivation, morale, and performance by creating a sense of identity and self to the project for followers, as well as a collective identity with the organization.

These leaders offer a role model that inspires, interests, and challenges their followers to take greater ownership for their work. A transformational leader understands the strengths and weaknesses of each follower and assigns tasks that enhance each individual's performance.

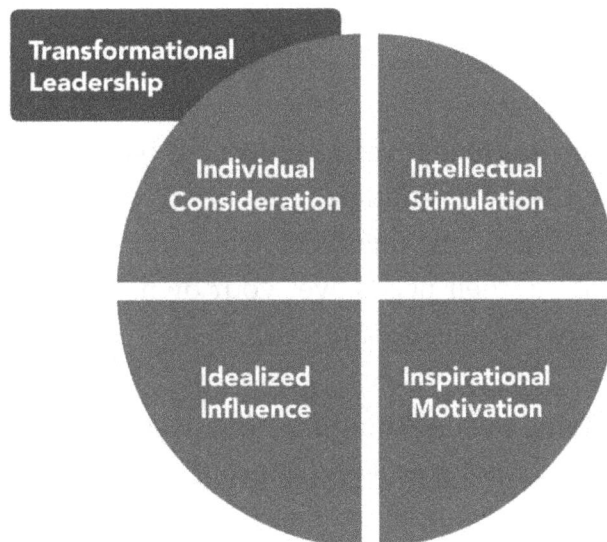

As a result, followers feel trust, admiration, loyalty, and respect for the leader, which means they are willing to put in whatever effort is required to achieve the goal, not just to gain benefit for themselves. There are four elements of transformational leadership:

1. Individualized Consideration—as leader you mentor your team, rewarding creativity and innovation. You actively listen to concerns and needs, offering support and empathy. You treat and challenge members according to their talents and knowledge, recognizing their contribution. You maintain open communications and empower your members to make decisions and support them as they are implemented. This helps member self-development and their intrinsic motivation.

2. Intellectual Stimulation—your leadership encourages innovation, looks for better ways to execute tasks, and challenges previous assumptions, thereby nurturing independent thinking. You encourage new ideas without criticism and see the unexpected as a learning opportunity.

3. Inspirational Motivation—this forms the foundation of your transformational leadership in the promotion to your members of a consistent vision or mission, which is so compelling and understandable that members know what they want from every interaction. It offers them a set of values that provide a sense of meaning and challenge that is motivational. Members work enthusiastically as a team and are committed to invest considerable effort in order to attain their tasks, having a firm belief in their abilities.

4. Idealized Influence—as leader your influence is based on members seeing you as a role model they want to emulate. They view you as someone who practices what you preach. This gains members' trust and respect, as they see that your ethical conduct places their needs over your own. This shows that you and your team strive to attain organizational goals.

Transformational leadership is something that many people aspire to, and the idea of being a truly inspirational leader is very appealing. The problem is that it can be difficult to implement in a competitive and unforgiving workplace where team members are working to tight deadlines and where any mistakes would have serious consequences.

The prevailing culture of your organization and the extent to which it values the development of managerial leadership skills will affect the practical application of this leadership style.

Applied to the Team Examples

The truth is that whilst this style of leadership is the subject of countless leadership courses and seminars, its practical application is very limited. Most managers will be judged on this quarter's performance figures or whether a particular project has been delivered on time and within budget.

Development Team

As a manager of the Development Team you will be able to utilize some of the aspects of transformational leadership, but you will be limited by the fact that not all of your team come from within the IT department—25% are seconded to you, and 38% come from outside the organization.

You may be able to assist in others achieving their personal goals but you will not be their only role model. As project manager, your performance will almost certainly be assessed in terms of the successful and timely completion of the project rather than from a staff development standpoint.

Customer Support Team

The nature of the routine and stressful work, plus the lack of opportunity for personal aspirations to be attained makes it difficult to see how this style of leadership can be incorporated into your Customer Support Team.

With virtually no promotion prospects, members see little opportunity or requirement for personal development, so adopting this style of leadership would be counterproductive for you as manager. This may seem harsh but it does reflect the reality of many low- level and poorly paid jobs.

Steering Team

As manager of the Steering Team your whole raison d'être is to investigate innovative and often revolutionary ideas, which may change the direction of the organization. For example:

- The sale of expertise to developing countries
- The setting up of a separate software company
- Breaking into new markets, e.g. insurance
- Acquisition of other utility companies
- Acquisition of suppliers, etc.

It is not difficult to imagine transformational leadership working well in the environment of a steering team as all four of the elements are both necessary and desirable if team members are to fully explore radical changes and approaches to the current business model. The majority of, if not all, members see their participation in your team as furthering their self-development and career progression.

Key Points

- Transformational leadership is based on the ability of the leader to offer a role model that inspires their followers to take greater ownership for their work.
- A transformational leader understands the strengths and weaknesses of each follower and assigns tasks that enhance each individual's performance.
- There are four elements of transformational leadership: Individualized Consideration, Intellectual Stimulation, Inspirational Motivation and Idealized In- fluence.

- It can be difficult to implement in a competitive and unforgiving workplace where team members are working to tight deadlines.

Situational Leadership

In contrast to the static nature of the environment required for both transactional and transformational leadership, you may find the ethos behind Situational Leadership better suited to the needs of your day-to-day team management.

The Situational Leadership model was developed in the early 1980s by Ken Blanchard and Paul Hersey. This model states that there is no single style of leadership that is effective in all circumstances.

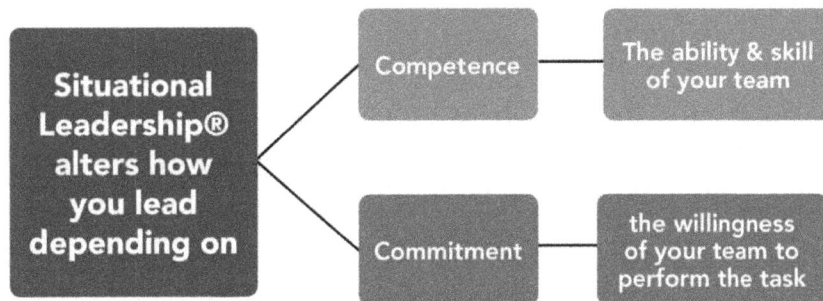

The most successful leaders and managers adapt their leadership style depending on the 'competence' and 'commitment' of the group, team, or individual being led.

As a manager you would alter your style to suit the ability of your team whether high or low (Competence) combined with the willingness or motivation of the team to do the task (Commitment), which is also either high or low. This offers you four possible combinations of what the model refers to as Maturity Levels (M1-4). These are listed below, together with a brief explanation about how a team at this level operates.

1. Maturity Level 1 (M1) – Low Competence/Skill & High Commitment/Will Your team would lack the ability to do the task you set them, but the members would be enthusiastic and willing to overcome this in order to complete the task.

2. Maturity Level 2 (M2) – Low Competence/Skill & Low Commitment/Will At this level your team would still lack the ability to do the task, but the members would display no enthusiasm or willingness to overcome this lack of knowledge

3. Maturity Level 3 (M3) – High Competence/Skill & Low Commitment/Will This team is capable of performing the task but shows no willingness to actually do it.

4. Maturity Level 4 (M4) – High Competence/Skill & High Commitment/Will This is a desirable team, as it is both able to complete the task and displays an enthusiasm and willingness to do so.

Within these four options at any one time, whether you look at the maturity levels vertically or horizontally, there is always a constant. On the vertical axis the level of skill is constant and on the horizontal axis the level of willingness is constant, whether you look at the top or bottom pair.

These Maturity Levels are also task-specific. So if you ask a team that normally has a maturity level M4 (High Skill / High Will) to perform a task it do not have the skills for it will have a maturity level M1 (Low Skill / High Will) for that particular task, and you will have to adapt your leadership accordingly.

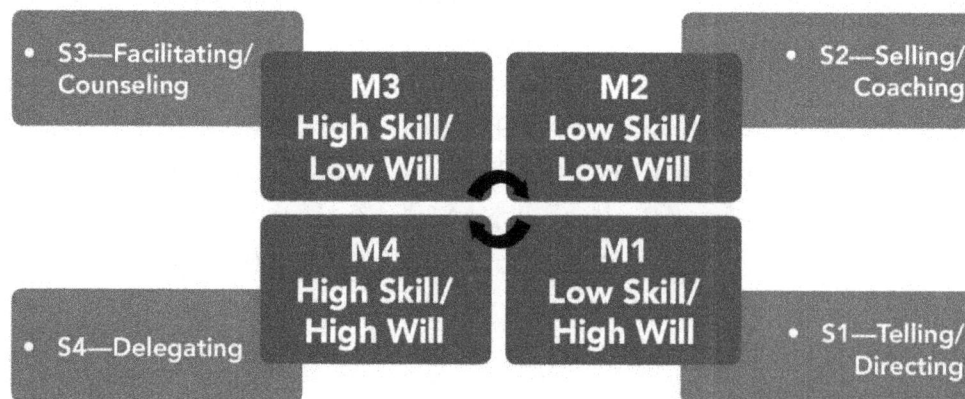

94

For each 'M' (Maturity) level there is a most effective leadership style you can adopt. This style not only suits the team or person you are managing but the task, role, or function that is required. The Situational Leadership® model suggests that there are four leadership styles (S1 to S4), which map onto the maturity levels (M1 to M4) of the team respectively.

1. Leadership Style S1 — Telling and Directing for M1 (Low Skill & High Will) To successfully manage this type of team you harness the team's enthusiasm to overcome their lack of knowledge. You would need to give explicit instructions throughout the task, telling your members exactly what their roles are, plus how and when to accomplish the task.

2. Leadership Style S2 — Selling and Coaching for M2 (Low Skill & Low Will) With this type of team you need to 'sell the task' and actively communicate with the members to provide the necessary information. You must provide the direction and the emotional support that will influence the team sufficiently to buy into the process, and be motivated to complete it.

3. Leadership Style S3 — Facilitating and Counselling for M3 (High Skill / Low Will) Managing this team requires you to focus more on the relationship, sharing the decision-making and motivating the team to accomplish the task. Your team possesses the necessary skills but lacks the willingness to actually do it.

4. Leadership Style S4 — Delegating for M4 (High Skill / High Will) Your role with this team is to monitor progress, allowing the members to use their ability and enthusiasm to manage the process and decision-making in order to complete the task.

Applied to the Team Examples

You can see that leadership styles S1 and S2 are best suited to situations where the focus is on getting the task done. But if your circumstances are more concerned with developing team members' abilities to work independently, leadership styles S3 and S4 are the ones you need to adopt.

For each of our team examples you would adopt the leadership style best suited to its function and situation.

Development Team

For this team, leadership style S4-M4 would be most appropriate as the team is well motivated and all of the team members are keen to add another successful project to their resumes.

Your role as manager is mainly one of monitoring, but in some instances or for certain individuals you may need to alter to S1-M1 if the skill levels require such a change. For example, you could be asked to join another project team that is mired in problems for a few weeks. You might then ask a competent member of you team to stand in for you, but whilst they are technically skilled they lack the experience of project management

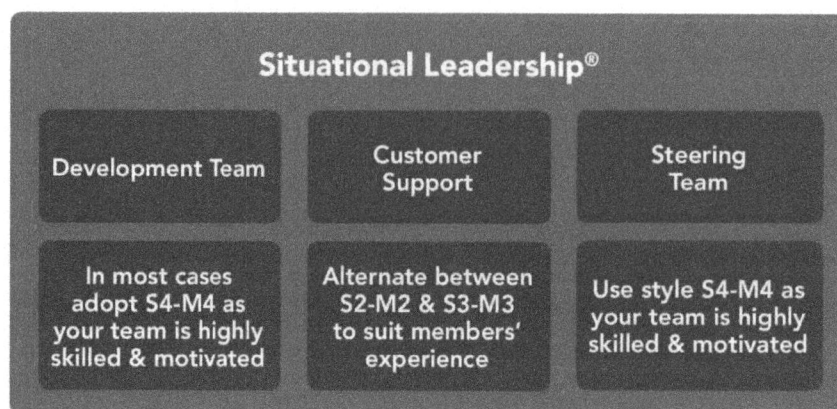

Customer Support Team

As Customer Support Manager you will have to be more adaptive in your leadership style as in most instances it will relate more to the individual than the task. You will probably find that for the majority of your time you oscillate between styles S2-M2 with your newer members who have low skill and little motivation, and style S3-M3 as you try to ensure your more experienced members participate, and try to motivate them to perform well.

Steering Team

Your management style for the Steering Team is almost certainly S4-M4 as your whole team comprises highly skilled and knowledgeable individuals who are all extremely self- motivated. These individuals need you to encourage and promote creativity to ensure that innovative and sound business decisions result from the team's activities. Situational Leadership® shows you that your team will be most successful when you adapt your leadership style to suit the team and situation. There is no one style that is optimal for you to use all the time. As an effective leader you need to be flexible and adapt yourself to the situation.

Key Points

- The Situational Leadership model states that there is no single style of leadership that is effective in all circumstances.
- It suggests that you should alter your leadership style to suit the ability and motivation of the team to do the task.

The Leadership Continuum

The final approach you can use is to ensure that your leadership arises out of the information you know about the task and members of your team. This approach is similar to Situational Leadership® in that it does not see leadership as a static state, but one that alters along a continuum so that your behaviour best suits the situation you are dealing with.

In 1958 Tannenbaum and Schmidt wrote of the Leadership Continuum for the first time. It describes a continuum of possible leadership behaviour available to you as a manager, along which many leadership styles may be placed. This offers you flexibility to adapt your leadership style to suit the situations you face every day at work.

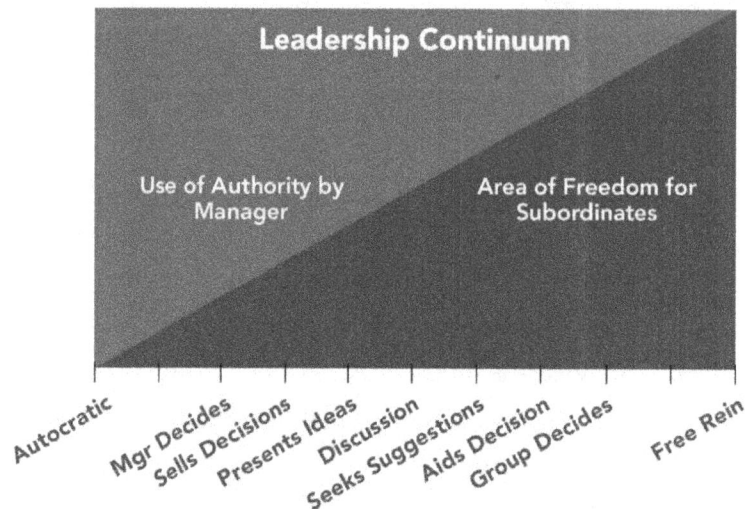

The continuum shows a range of actions that relate to the degree of authority used by the team leader and to the amount of freedom available to your members in arriving at decisions.

At one extreme there is 'autocratic,' often referred to as 'Boss-Centered' leadership, where you as manager would have total authority to make decisions and announce these to your team. This is unlikely to exist in your workplace because your decisions will frequently have to be made after consultation with senior management or shareholders, sometimes both.

As a manager or leader you are characterized according to the degree of control that you retain in the decision-making process. The four styles of leadership are known as 'Tells' (for the autocratic leader), then 'Sells', followed by 'Consults,' and finally 'Delegates.'

Tells Sells Consults Delegates

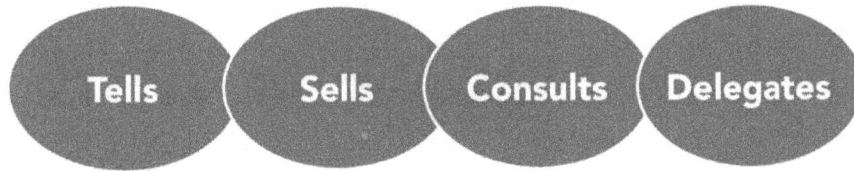

You may work in an environment that requires you to resolve problems and inform your team of what they must do to address these problems without any consultation. In this instance you would be using the 'Tells' style of leadership within the continuum. Alternatively, your team may need to be persuaded by you to accept your decision before they will act. In this case you would adopt a 'Sells' style.

As the situation you work in evolves, your leadership style may move further along the continuum and you will be able to alter your style to that of 'Consults.' Your style becomes that of a facilitator: you present the problem to your team to resolve and the decision is jointly owned. The final style on the leadership continuum is known as 'Delegates.' This is where you define the framework your team works within to resolve a problem without interference.

The three factors that will help your decide which leadership style to adopt along the continuum are your own personality, the team itself, and the environment you are working in. Your own values, knowledge, and experience will influence your selection of a style.

The second factor affecting your chosen style will be the composition, character, distribution of skills, knowledge, and attitude of your members. You need to ask yourself whether or not your members are willing and able to accept responsibility for decision making. You will also need to assess how well they identify with and comprehend your organization's goals.

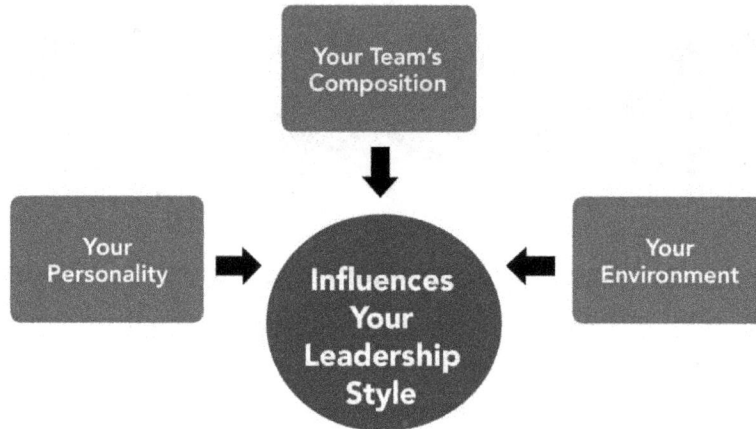

The third and final factor is the environment you find yourself working in. This is made up of three aspects: the type and ethos of your organization, the nature of the problem you face, and the timescales within which it needs to be resolved.

According to the continuum theory, as leaders become more successful they learn to recognize and then portray the most appropriate behaviour to suit the circumstances they face.

Applying this Style to the Team Examples

The most likely leadership style you would adopt along the continuum for each of our team examples would be:

Development Team

Your selected leadership style would be heavily dictated by the experience of your team. With a more experienced team you would be able to adopt a 'Consults' style where you present the problem and act as a facilitator in discussions to arrive at a jointly owned decision.

With a less experienced team you would adapt your style to 'Sells,' persuading your members to accept your decision using your more extensive experience to break down their resistance and hesitancy resulting from a lack of knowledge.

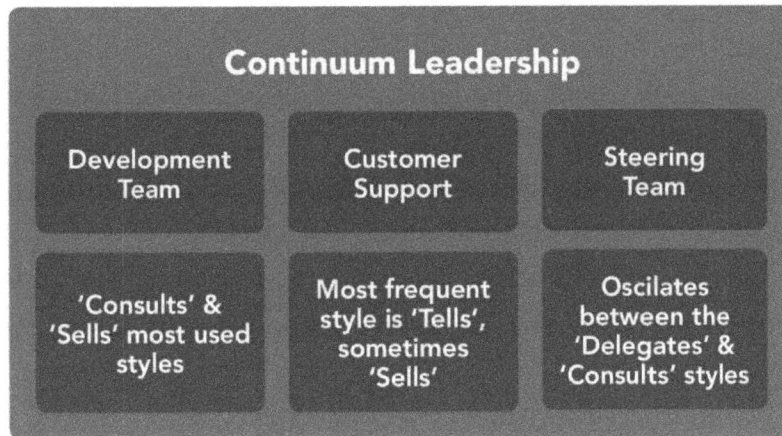

Continuum Leadership

Development Team	Customer Support	Steering Team
'Consults' & 'Sells' most used styles	Most frequent style is 'Tells', sometimes 'Sells'	Oscilates between the 'Delegates' & 'Consults' styles

Customer Support Team

As manager of this team you are most likely going to lead using a 'Tells' style. This is because you will identify a problem (often from reviewing the call statistics), come up with a solution, and then announce to your members what they need to do. Your members will not be involved in the decision-making process or the timescale.

At other times you may be able to adapt to a 'Sells' style where you persuade your team to accept your decision and act accordingly.

Steering Team

The nature and composition of your team allows you as manager to use a leadership style of 'Delegates.' The investigation of the Steering Team defines the parameters your team must work within, and you need to allow them to work within those limits without interference.

Often within this type of team you will have some sub-groups that require more guidance. In these instances you would adopt a 'Consults' style where you present the problem to your team and facilitate a shared solution.

Key Points

- This approach suggests that leadership behaviour should change to best suit the situation you are dealing with.
- The four styles of leadership are known as 'Tells' (for the autocratic leader), then 'Sells', followed by 'Consults,' and finally 'Delegates.'
- The three factors that will help your decide which leadership style to adopt along the continuum are your own personality, the team itself, and the environment you are working in.

Summary

Over the last 40 years, dozens of leadership theories have been published by academics or by management consultancies looking to create a proprietary leadership method from which they can then make money. As a result, there is a huge body of work available on leadership, much of which makes the claim that this is the latest approach, the most scientific approach, the most effective approach, and so on.

If you decide to study the available information on leadership, then you should do so knowing that most of what you read is simply a rehash of existing theories with some unique selling point or 'spin' grafted on in order to turn it into a saleable method.

In addition, most books on leadership can't resist the temptation to deal with this topic as if every manager really did have the potential to become the next Steve Jobs or Bill Gates. Whilst this might make for a thrilling read, it is usually quite difficult for you to apply any of the advice given unless you're on the board of directors or are working for a small organization where you really do have a lot of influence and authority.

For you as a manager, the most important aspect of your leadership is deciding how much freedom to give your team. Too much, and they may not achieve their targets, too little, and you will restrict their personal development and job satisfaction which can cause problems with motivation and productivity.

There is no easy answer to this problem and the best course of action is to consider each case on its merits with a clear appreciation of the risks involved of giving too much autonomy.

Preface

Rebuilding an underperforming team can be a huge challenge. This eBook explains why teams underperform and provides practical advice about how to identify and fix performance problems.

You will learn:

- The four essential behaviours you must demonstrate in order to turn around an underperforming team.
- How to deal with the problems inherent in matrix or cross-functional teams where you do not have authority over all of the team members
- The six 'silent barriers' to performance that cannot be tackled directly because they result from issues that senior management prefers to ignore.
- How to recognize the symptoms of GroupThink and prevent it from becoming a problem in your team.
- How to stop Ingroup behaviour having an adverse effect on your team's performance and reputation within the organization.

Introduction

All teams experience difficulties from time to time and it is your responsibility as a man- ager to resolve any problems as quickly as possible. Some team problems can be traced to an individual team member who is not performing as expected or who is causing conflict within the team. Understanding what motivates people, as well as why they become disenchanted with their work will enable you to address these types of problem.

However, sometimes the lack of progress, poor productivity, or interpersonal conflict is not the fault of any one team member but is down to the way that the team is organized and managed. Proper goal setting, clear role definition, and having the necessary pro- cesses in place to deal with the day-to-day management of the team are all important, as is your ability to anticipate problems and identify the early signs of underperformance.

What is actually meant by an 'underperforming' team? Any full explanation would need to include specific details that relate to the exact situation and environment of the poorly performing team. But in general terms what is meant by underperformance can be summarized in the following sentence:

An individual, team, division, or corporation is said to be 'underperforming' when their actual achievements fall below the level of performance required or a predefined objective is not attained.

For the majority of managers the required level of achievement is defined in your annual appraisal and should tie into your organization's mission. Your level of performance should be regularly monitored so that any aspect of poor performance does not come as a surprise to either you or your manager.

You should be regularly assessing, measuring, and reporting back to your team so that they know how well they are performing. The earlier you can isolate problems the sooner you can look for ways to resolve them.

There has been a lot of academic study into the reasons why teams underperform and some of this work is directly applicable to the types of team that you will find yourself re- sponsible for. These are: Herzberg's Hygiene Theory, Hackman's work on leading teams, and the Six Silent Barriers of Beer et al. An understanding of this research will help you to understand why it is that teams underperform and what you can do about it.

In addition, many project teams find themselves operating in a 'Matrix Management Environment,' which can create a specific set of problems that the project manager or team leader needs to be aware of from project inception.

Finally, there are two types of negative behaviour that can develop when a group of people are working closely together. These can be very destructive because the team appears to be working well together and problems may not be obvious until it is too late to do anything about them.

This Book describes all of these reasons why teams underperform and provides practical advice about how to identify and fix performance problems.

Herzberg's hygiene Theory

The first piece of research that interests us was undertaken by Fredrick Herzberg in 1959 to investigate 'satisfaction at work.' The result of this research became known as Herzberg's Hygiene Theory (or the Two Factor Theory) and showed that those factors that gave a person satisfaction at work and those that resulted in dissatisfaction are quite different in nature.

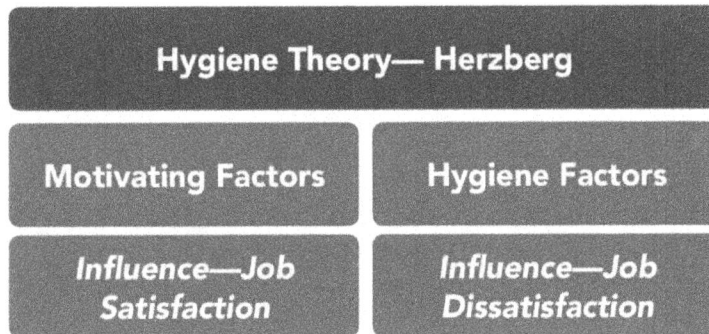

Herzberg referred to those things that influenced job satisfaction as 'Motivating Factors,' whilst he called those that influenced dissatisfaction at work 'Hygiene Factors.'

Motivating factors include: achievement, recognition, challenge, responsibility, promotion, and personal growth. As a manager, you can improve a team member's satisfaction in their work by making positive changes to the work itself, for example by providing opportunities to achieve goals or take on more responsibility

To prevent dissatisfaction you should focus your efforts on hygiene factors. These include things like salary, benefits, job security, working conditions, supervision, company policy, procedures, and relationships with co-workers.

His findings showed that these two sets of factors act independently of each other and that increasing your team's satisfaction level will not automatically lead to a lower level of dissatisfaction. For example, if a team member is not motivated by the goals they are set then this problem will not go away simply because they are given a pay rise.

This is because the increased level of pay quickly becomes the norm. The same thing applies to improvements in working conditions, better relationships within their team, or any of the other hygiene factors already mentioned.

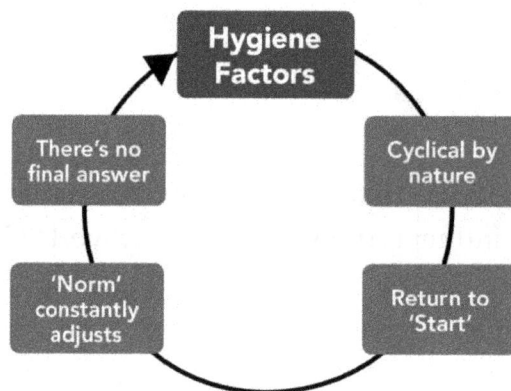

The cyclical nature of these hygiene factors means that you cannot reap the benefit of improving any of them for very long. The best that you can hope for is to keep the dissatisfaction at a sufficiently low level to avoid excessive staff turnover and absenteeism.

You can only make a lasting positive impact on your team's attitude by working on both hygiene factors and motivating factors together on an ongoing basis.

If you inherit a poorly performing team when you take on a new role or join a new organization your first action should be to identify the negative factors causing poor performance. You can then assess how easily you can alter the hygiene factors and what changes to make to the motivating factors, because to make any real changes in performance you need to address both.

Key Points

- Herzberg's Hygiene Theory shows that the factors that result in satisfaction at work and those that result in dissatisfaction are quite different in nature.
- Motivating factors include: achievement, recognition, challenge, responsibility, promotion, and personal growth.
- To prevent dissatisfaction you should focus your efforts on things like salary, benefits, job security, working conditions, supervision, company policy, procedures, and relationships with co-workers.

Leading Teams—hackman

J. Richard Hackman, a Harvard University Professor of Social and Organizational Psychology, has spent his career analyzing team effectiveness. His research has shown that more often than not people work less effectively than one would expect. In many cases, team members have difficulty agreeing on the purpose of the team and the issues of coordination and motivation within the team erode the potential benefits gained from collaboration.

Hackman believes that a successful team usually has a disciplined and committed manager who determinedly sets the team goal, allows the team to select their own members and then define their own structure and processes. Unfortunately, this approach is rarely possible for you as a manager. In the real world senior management decide on a team's membership, and their reasoning for including certain individuals may be influenced by politics or simply by who is available.

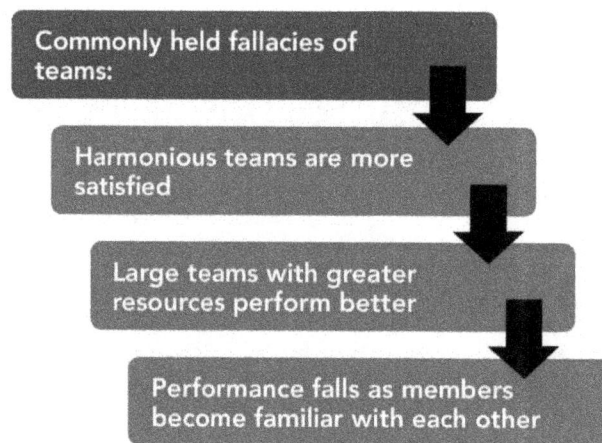

In their recent research, Hackman and his colleagues James Burruss, Debra Nunes, and Ruth Wageman were able to disprove certain beliefs often associated with teams that perform well:

- Harmonious teams are more satisfied in their work
- Larger teams with greater resources perform better
- Performance falls off as team members become more familiar with each other

In their book, Senior Leadership Teams, they explain that even though teams may not be totally harmonious the members can still feel satisfied after performing a task well and receiving recognition for it. They found that the satisfaction orchestra members felt after playing had more to do with how well their performance was received than how the members felt about playing together.

Larger teams may have greater resources at their disposal, but they also have a far greater number of potential communication paths between members. As a manager you will find that as the size of the team you have to manage increases, so does the occurrence of disruptions and conflicts between members. Hackman and his fellow researchers recommend that team numbers remain in single digits, although this is not always possible with workplace teams.

The third misconception that Hackman and his team dispelled was the belief that newer teams outperform well-established ones. There is a lot of research that shows that performance does not fall off as the team members become more familiar and comfortable with each other. A study conducted by NASA showed that fatigued or tired crews that had a history of working as a team made around half the errors of a team made up of fresh pilots who had not flown together before.

Key Points

- The issues of coordination and motivation within a team can erode the potential benefits gained from collaboration.
- Hackman's research suggests that there are some commonly held fallacies about teams and that smaller teams who are familiar with each other often outperform larger teams with no experience of working together.

Six Silent Barriers — Beer et al.

Mike Beer, a Professor of Business Administration at the Harvard Business School, has identified six 'silent barriers' that cause teams to underperform.

People working within the organization recognize these barriers, but they cannot be tackled because they result from issues that senior management prefers to ignore

1	Unclear strategy & values, conflicting priorities
2	Ineffective senior team
3	Leader style too top-down or laissez faire
4	Poor horizontal coordination & communication
5	Poor leadership, management skills & development
6	Poor or closed vertical communication

These Silent barriers are:
1. Unclear strategy and values, and conflicting priorities
2. An ineffective senior team
3. Leadership style is too top-down or too laissez faire
4. Poor horizontal coordination and communications
5. Inadequate leadership, management skills and development in the organization
6. Poor or closed vertical communications

Beer says,

'In organizations that exhibit these barriers, you see that the leadership team members are coming with their own agenda, and there is no effective senior team in place that is committed to the same strategy, priorities and values. The lower levels don't know what the top is trying to do and upper levels don't know what they want done. And there is silence; the lower level teams can't speak honestly with the top about what the problems are that block their efficacy – clear and common priorities and strategy or their pattern of management.'

Beer's conclusions are based on the work he and his colleagues have completed with several organizations, using a method called the Strategic Fitness Process, which utilizes organizations' employees as 'researchers.' In their work, Beer and his colleagues ask senior management teams to define their strategic direction in a two or three-page statement and to appoint a task force of 8-10 people who will go out and interview 100 employees across all parts of the organization.

Beer believes that solving the problems that these barriers create is the main issue for many managers. The process of reviewing and setting priorities is a continual one, which with careful monitoring shows when and where adjustments need to be made to ensure teams perform well.

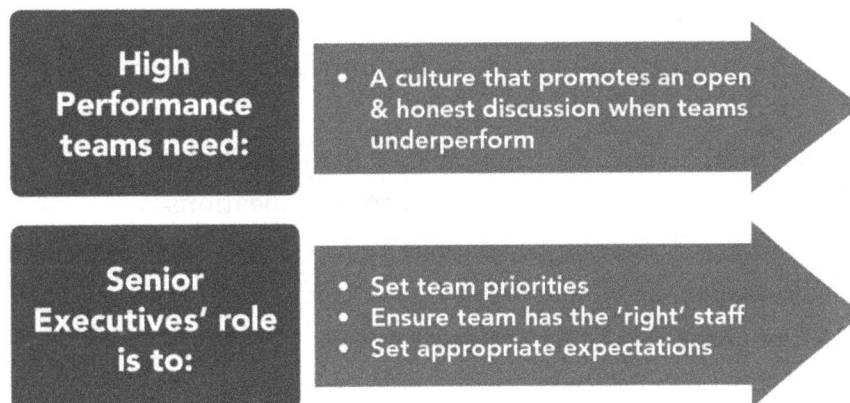

High Performance teams need:	• A culture that promotes an open & honest discussion when teams underperform
Senior Executives' role is to:	• Set team priorities • Ensure team has the 'right' staff • Set appropriate expectations

Without these changes coming from the top levels organizations that have cross-functional teams will continue to be ineffective and show poor performance. This is especially true for global corporations where the need to coordinate across different business and geographic regions is essential.

Ultimately, senior management should aim to create a culture that allows constructive discussion on difficult issues without the need to find 'someone to blame.' To achieve this, the executive needs to define priorities, ensure the right employees are assigned to the right teams, and ensure that each team knows what is expected of it.

The findings of these research studies illustrate that some team performance problems may originate from cultural factors that you have no control over. Nonetheless, being aware of these issues should help you to understand why a team may be underperforming despite your best efforts.

Key Points

- Mike Beer has identified six 'silent barriers' that cause teams to underperform.
- These barriers cannot be tackled because they result from issues that senior management prefers to ignore.
- These silent barriers are:
  - Unclear strategy and values, and conflicting priorities
  - An ineffective senior team
  - Leadership style is too top-down or too laissez faire
  - Poor horizontal coordination and communications
  - Inadequate leadership, management skills and development in the organization
  - Poor or closed vertical communications

Why do Teams Underperform?

Many of the factors highlighted by Herzberg, Hackman, and Beer are not things that you as a manager have direct control over. For example, you will need to work within existing organizational policy with regard to working conditions; your executive may not be prepared to adopt a culture where 'silent barriers' can be openly discussed; and you may not be able to respond to market pay increases when you have a defined salary/bonus budget.

However, there are some general symptoms that you can watch out for as manager. These will indicate that your team, or a member, is not performing as well as you would expect.

- Absences from the team and its activities that are lengthy and cannot be explained
- More frequent displays of conflict and frustration, often unjustified
- Lack of enthusiasm and motivation to perform tasks
- Rumors and gossip heard on the organization's grapevine about your team are on the increase
- A clique develops so that these people protect themselves from the stigma of poor performance

You will need to be constantly monitoring and observing how each of your team members is performing and look for signs of reduced productivity. Assessing how well your team's performance compares to other teams in your organization is also an essential part of your role. If you notice a reduction in performance, understanding why this has occurred and addressing it are essential.

The most common reasons teams or individuals underperform are:

- Lack of clarity and focus
- Lack of ability
- Lack of confidence
- Lack of direction
- Lack of motivation

Lack of Clarity and Focus

If team members keep on asking exactly what they should be doing, by when, and how they should actually perform the task then this indicates that their responsibilities have not been specified clearly enough.

This type of behaviour may also imply that they need more feedback from you so that they understand how well you want them to do the job. Many jobs can be expanded to fit the time available, and you should regularly review the team's work to prevent this from happening. It is quite common to see team members spending a lot of time 'perfecting' things that don't really need it rather than doing an adequate job and then moving on to another task. For example, if a team member is preparing a document for use within the team, then you might consider accepting a less polished format than if it was going to be more widely circulated.

Lack of Ability

One of your members, or the team itself, may be underperforming because they have been assigned a task that they are not skilled or knowledgeable enough to undertake.

To prevent this situation arising, you should have an appreciation of each team member's capabilities. You can assess how much additional training and coaching you can offer to help develop their skills, but in the end you need to make a judgment on how well their skills match the task requirements. This inability to perform the task may also be due to a lack of resources, whether it be in terms of people, materials, or funds.

In your role as team leader you need to ensure that higher levels of management are made aware of the skill level of your team, manage their expectations of what tasks your team can accomplish, and feed back when constraints exist.

Finally, to ensure you only have capable members added to your team you should take an active role in the selection and induction of new members.

Lack of Confidence

Your team may find itself performing a new role or task following a reorganization or merger. This may result in a lower level of performance as the change causes the team to lose confidence in their abilities to handle the new tasks and processes.

Sometimes as a manager you will notice that an individual, despite having the right qualifications, just doesn't seem to perform as well as you expected. This can be because they don't possess the required behavioural skills, or they lack the interest to adjust and learn the new skills that are necessary for their role.

This person could also just not fit into the social make-up of your team even though they have the right skills. In this instance often the individual begins to feel unappreciated, and they may even feel ostracized by the rest of the team. As a consequence their performance declines, and the situation deteriorates because the rest of the team resent carrying an underperformer.

Lack of Direction

This is probably one of the most common reasons for underperformance. As a manager you should make certain that the goal and task descriptions you provide are as clear as possible. For more information on this topic you should see our eBook 'Personal Productivity—Effective Goal Setting,' which can be accessed in series by Management Sage.

If your own goals are poorly defined it will not help the performance of your team. This could be due to one of the 'silent barriers' described by Beer and his team of researchers. Often this results from senior management having hidden agendas, which undermine performance and bring about a culture of mistrust.

Lack of Motivation

Some of your team may just not care about doing a good job, and they may even avoid working altogether. This lack of motivation can have a variety of causes, including personal problems, lack of career development opportunities, and increased pressure be- cause of reduced resources.

Motivating your team will often be handled as part of their appraisal system, but this is not enough in itself. You also need to be monitoring and feeding back to each individual how well he or she is doing on an ongoing basis. If the team is involved in boring or repetitive work then motivation may be your number one priority.

Key Points

- The most common reasons teams or individuals underperform are: lack of clarity and focus, lack of ability, lack of confidence, lack of direction and lack of motivation.

Matrix Management Issues

Many managers find themselves operating in a 'Matrix Management Environment.' Matrix or Cross-Functional management is a technique of managing people through a series of dual-reporting relationships instead of a more traditional linear management structure

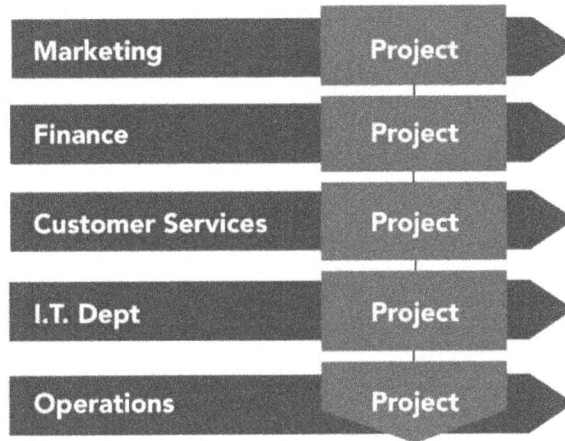

This style of management is popular in highly collaborative projects that bring individuals from functional departments (e.g. marketing, customer services, finance, etc.) into the project team. This means that most of the project members operate under a dual authority system—they report to their own line manager as well as the project manager.

For you as the project manager this means that you will have to ensure your communication channels between you and the line managers are effective. In addition, appreciating that the line managers' priorities are often going to be different to those of your project will help you when discussing the availability of resources. If not handled properly, this has the potential for conflict and confusion, which will inevitably lead to a decrease in performance.

One key aspect of maintaining your team's performance in this matrix structure is getting the 'right' resources at the time required by the plan. If your team members are willing but lack the necessary skills to perform their project role then the whole team's performance will decline.

The success of the matrix team structure is reliant on senior management's support for the project and for establishing the correct procedures and processes that support this type of environment.

Key Points

- Matrix management is a technique of managing people through a series of dual-reporting relationships instead of a more traditional linear management structure.
- This means that some team members operate under a dual authority system — they report to their own line manager as well as the project manager.

Turning Underperformance around

Warren Bennis is an American scholar, organizational consultant, and author, widely regarded as a pioneer of the contemporary field of Leadership Studies. He has written approximately 30 books on leadership. Bennis believes that the only way to get the best performance from your team is through your own behaviour.

Does your behaviour display that you know where you are going and why it is important that you get there?

Does it show that you care for each member of your team, the team as a whole, and attaining the team goal?

Bennis refers to four behaviours managers must become competent in to be good leaders. These are management of attention, meaning, trust, and self.

- Attention — sum up goals in a way team can buy into
- Meaning — clearly state aims and priorities
- Trust — build rapport and open, honest communication
- Self — lead by example

Bennis says that only when someone has learnt these competencies will they be able to display them in their behaviour and become a good leader.

A common element of such behaviour is the ability to communicate clearly and concisely with others. Good communication, whether verbal or written, should remove any uncertainty by using the S.S.U. principle in all exchanges

Good Communicators:

Use Straightforward language

Make requests Specific

Check for Understanding

This means that you communicate with others by making your requests very specific, use straightforward language free of jargon and ambiguity and finally check that you have been clearly understood. By communicating in this way you will ensure that your team is confident of your direction and that you care about them.

Learning Your Team's History

Before you can make real progress with your team you need to appreciate what has gone on before you became their manager. This will take time and requires you to build up trust so that individuals can be honest in answering your questions.

Using your organization's appraisal system with its regular progress meetings will help develop this trust with your team as they can be assured of the confidentiality of your discussions. Over time you will build up a rapport with each member that encourages them to perform to the best of their ability.

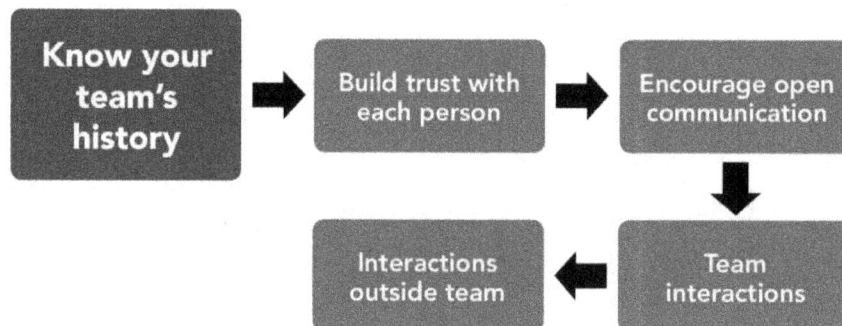

You also need to understand the nature of past interactions outside of the group, both within the organization and with external parties. By identifying any problems in this area you can begin to rebuild respect and understanding in these relations so that future relations have a positive impact on your team's performance.

By understanding what has gone before you can get a true picture of what steps you need to take to restore the self-esteem and motivation of your team. You demonstrate through your own behaviour that you will seek answers to their problems and coach them how best to meet their targets.

For example, the week after bills are sent out your Customer Support Team always com- plain of irate customers calling back because their replacement bill hasn't arrived the following day as promised. On investigation you discover this is because the system only reprints bills once a week. Letting your members know of this process means that they can then inform the customers appropriately and avoid setting unrealistic expectations.

Know Your Team

By investigating the history of your team you can discover how successful previous managers have been in establishing incentives to motivate the team and how well each member's abilities match their role. Many books on leadership tell you that by carefully choosing the members of your team, problems of lack of ability and motivation are resolved! You will rarely come across situations where you can do this, however, because you will usually have to work with the team you are given or inherit.

Your first action should be to understand each of your members in terms of the abilities they have now, their likely potential, how motivated they are, and if there is anything that will motivate them further. There will only be certain issues you can influence, for example guidance, support, coaching, and recognition. So try to avoid discussing things that you have no control over, such as pay structures or organizational policy.

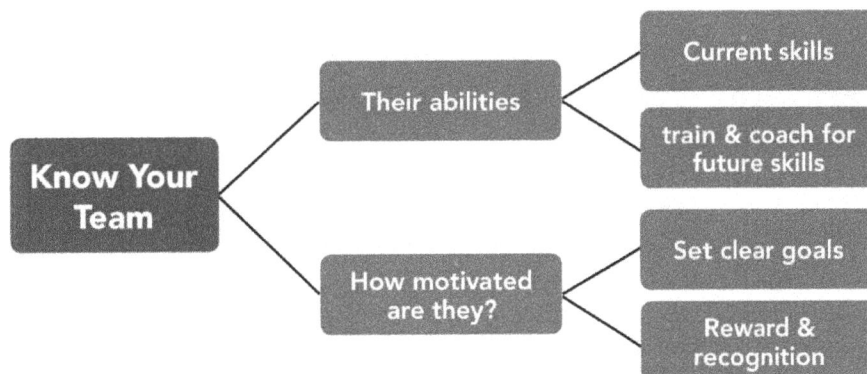

You can use the appraisal process to your advantage by conducting short quarterly or monthly reviews of progress with your team members to not only monitor how well they are performing but also to gain valuable information about any issues that they feel are holding them back. These issues may be due to a lack of integration within the team, and depending on the nature of your team you may find conducting Peer Evaluations an excellent way to discover the root causes and possible solutions.

You must first ensure that such an exercise is viewed in a constructive way and not seen as a witch-hunt. You will need to be explicit in your instructions so that everyone knows what is expected of them, how you will use the findings, and how you will communicate them to the team. For example, you may want to present the broad findings to the whole team and discuss how these affect performance, and then talk more specifically to individuals as part of the appraisal process

If you wish to involve your whole team in this process it is referred to as a 360° evaluation. Each member rates all other members of the team (including themselves and you as leader) against certain criteria of your choosing, with '1' being poor and '5' being excellent. Your criteria could be:

- How reliable is the person?
- Is the person a team player?
- Does the person show a positive attitude towards other team members?
- Are the person's skills a valuable asset to the team?
- Does the person show a positive attitude towards their work?
- Is this person someone you would be happy to have leading you?
- Does this person suggest innovative ideas that help the team?
- Is this person supportive of other members?
- Does this person carry their fair share of the workload?

All these ratings are done anonymously and the resulting spreadsheet indicates where each individual is strong and areas that need development. It will also show you the breadth of skill across the whole team and highlight any gaps you team may have.

For example, an individual may be seen by the majority of the team as someone they are happy to be led by, but from your other research you know that the person does not recognize this attribute in themselves. In this case, you have identified someone oth- ers are happy to follow, but who needs coaching and mentoring in order to achieve this leadership role.

This information will help you to come up with a development plan for each team member that enables him or her to work on their strengths. If you have the flexibility to alter roles within your team in accordance with what you have learnt about each person then this will help to maximize motivation and performance.

An equally important part of this process is to review the resources your team has to work with. Do they have the necessary systems and equipment they need to perform their role? For instance, in our Customer Support Team example you may be able to gain 'read only' access for the team to certain systems that enable them to give more informed answers to callers.

Key Points

Before you can make real progress with an underperforming team you need to appreciate what has gone on before you became their manager.

You also need to understand the nature of past interactions outside of the group, both within the organization and with external parties.

By investigating the history of your team you can discover how successful previous managers have been in establishing incentives to motivate the team and how well each member's abilities match their role.

This information will help you to come up with a development plan for each team member that enables him or her to work on their strengths.

Group Think and Ingroup Behaviour

GroupThink was a term coined in 1972 by Irving L. Janis, an American research psychologist and professor at the University of California. He described it as an observable fact that groups tend to ignore or discredit information that does not fit in with the group's ethos and beliefs. There are several famous historical events where GroupThink has been implicated. Two examples are Pearl Harbor and the Challenger Space Shuttle disaster.

In 1941, the Americans received several reports that the Japanese were preparing for an attack on Pearl Harbor. But as this was the headquarters of the US fleet and was believed to be secure these warnings were ignored. The result was that on December 7 the US fleet sustained extensive damage, with devastating numbers killed. The event brought the United States into World War II.

In 1986, the space shuttle Challenger broke apart 73 seconds into its flight, causing the deaths of its seven crew members. The Rogers Commission investigation found that NA- SA's organizational culture and decision-making processes had been key contributing factors to the accident.

They discovered that NASA managers had known about a potentially catastrophic flaw in the design of the rocket booster since 1977, but had failed to address it properly. The managers also disregarded warnings from engineers about the dangers posed by the low temperatures on the morning of the accident, and failed to adequately report these technical concerns to their superiors.

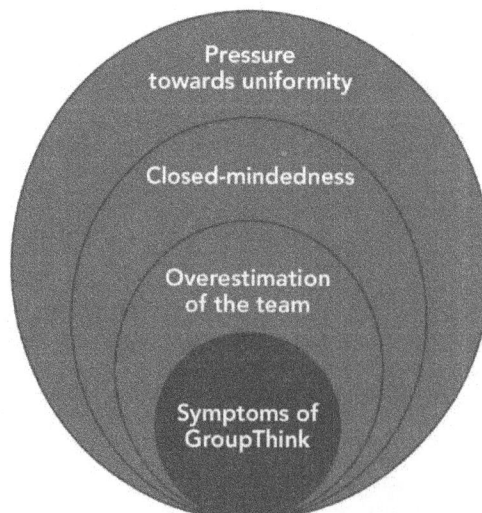

Such events are extreme examples of a situation where teams or groups of people felt that maintaining harmony and consensus within the group was more important than realistically appraising alternative courses of action. Janis identified three basic symptoms of Group Think:

Overestimations of the Team—the members believe that their moral code is high and as such anything they decide is good. This feeling of goodness also prevents fear of failure during a crisis.

Closed-mindedness—members construct rationalizations in order to discount warnings and other forms of negative feedback that, taken seriously, might lead group members to reconsider their assumptions. Team members view groups outside of their team in a negative way and this enables the team to minimize decision conflicts between ethical values and expediency.

Pressures toward Uniformity—members don't want to deviate from the consensus of the group so keep quiet about any misgivings they may have. This behaviour minimizes any doubts they have themselves, and they block from their minds any information that brings the group's beliefs into question. This silence is seen as acceptance, and any member expressing doubt comes under severe pressure to conform to the shared values.

As a manager you are mostly likely to come across the issue of Group Think if you are working in a highly cohesive team that is under considerable pressure to make a decision or meet a deadline. Such pressures can result in team members preferring to seek consensus rather than realistically appraise alternative courses of action.

This means that decisions made in this way by a Group Think team are unlikely to achieve a successful outcome. You should view Group Think as a continuum rather than some- thing that is either present or absent within a group or team. Remember, some disagreement is a good thing as it demonstrates that issues have been thoroughly debated prior to a decision being reached.

You also need to be mindful that if your team has been together for a long time, or has been through a stressful time, it may exhibit what sociologists refer to as the Ingroup/ Outgroup phenomenon. A primary purpose of team building is to create an 'ingroup'; this is perfectly reasonable, and helps the team to overcome internal differences in order to confront external problems.

However, one of the unintended consequences of this bias is that team members may come to view people outside of the team as an 'Outgroup,' towards which they feel contempt or opposition, or against which they desire to compete. If left unchecked, this behaviour can become very destructive and have an adverse effect on the team's performance. It can also damage the team's image and standing within the organization.

You will need to ensure that you educate and illustrate to the team their own and others' importance in achieving the organization's objectives. Your best approach in defeating GroupThink and Ingroup/Outgroup behaviours is to follow five steps.

Five steps to avoid GroupThink & Ingroup/Outgroup behaviors

⬇

1. Encourage members to challenge ideas & present objections

⬇

2. Seek ideas from those outside of the team

⬇

3. Invite outside experts to your meetings

⬇

4. Avoid expressing management's opinions on the desired outcome

⬇

5. Assign a person to engage others in testing quality of argument

These steps are:

1. Team leaders should encourage each member to challenge ideas and present objections.
2. Team members should talk to and solicit ideas from people outside the group
3. Outside experts should be invited to attend some team meetings.
4. Management should avoid expressing opinions about the preferred outcome.
5. Assign a Devil's Advocate at critical meetings. This person seeks to engage others in testing the quality of the original argument so any weaknesses can be identified. The original position is then either improved or abandoned.

Whether you inherit a team exhibiting GroupThink or InGroup/Outgroup behaviour, or you see the early signs of this behaviour becoming a pattern in your team, you need to create a working environment where openness, participation, and new ideas are encouraged and welcomed by all.

This stage of the process of turning your team around should not be rushed and can take up to 12 months to complete. Once you have developed your team so that they want to perform their tasks as well as have the right skills and knowledge to perform the tasks well, this will become a constant cycle of management activity.

Summary

Rebuilding an underperforming team can be a huge challenge. Occasionally, problems can be traced to an individual team member who is not performing as expected or who is causing conflict within the team. This issue is probably the easiest to deal with provided that the individual accepts that their behaviour is causing a problem and they are open to the idea of additional training or reassignment.

If on the other hand, you find yourself in a situation where there is widespread discontent then you should initially focus your efforts on so-called 'hygiene' factors. These include things like salary, benefits, job security, working conditions, supervision, company policy and organizational procedures.

You will need to ask yourself whether any of these are at odds with your industry norms. If they are then 'quick fix' solutions are unlikely to work, as team members will be feel that they have legitimate grievances that need to be addressed.

Some of these factors may be beyond your authority to improve but if you can make a compelling case to senior management then the underlying problems may not be insurmountable.

There may also be 'silent barriers' that cause teams to underperform. These barriers cannot be tackled directly because they result from issues that senior management prefers to ignore.

It can be very frustrating when team performance problems originate from cultural factors that you have no control over. Nonetheless, being aware of these issues should help you to understand why a team may be underperforming despite your best efforts.

Preface

This Book describes the ten most popular contemporary leadership theories and models. You can use these as inspiration and a potential toolkit from which you can develop your own leadership style based on your own personality, the task at hand and the team that you are leading.

It describes following leadership theories and models:

- Action Centred Leadership
- Blake-Mouton Managerial Grid
- Dunham and Pierce's Leadership Process Model
- Fiedler's Contingency Model
- French and Raven's Five Forms of Power
- Hersey-Blanchard Situational Leadership Theory
- Tannenbaum-Schmidt Leadership Continuum
- Lewin's Leadership Styles Framework
- Path-Goal Theory
- Zenger and Folkman's 10 Fatal Leadership Flaws

Introduction

The subject of Leadership has been studied for hundreds of years and reveals an evolving succession of theories. The earliest theories focus mostly on the character and personality of successful leaders and how they behaved. The more recent theories focus on what leaders actually do rather than on them needing to have certain innate qualities or traits.

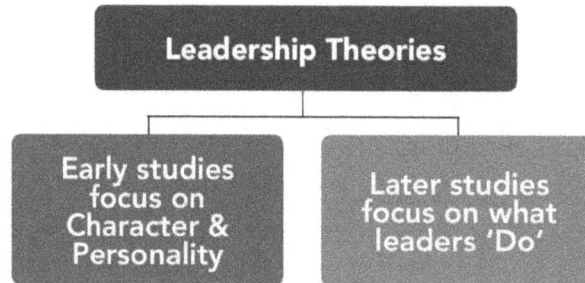

Leadership Theories

Early studies focus on Character & Personality

Later studies focus on what leaders 'Do'

Early trait theories attempted to create a list of leadership qualities and behaviours associated with 'good' leaders. They saw these aspects as what anyone who wanted to lead needed to possess to be successful. They derived that a leader must have six basic qualities or behavioural traits to be a leader. They are:

- Honesty & Integrity
- Emotional Maturity
- Motivation
- Self-confidence
- Cognitive Ability
- Achievement Drive

Many of histories great leaders, both military and political, had this type of persona personal but there have been some significant exceptions that have damaged such theories.

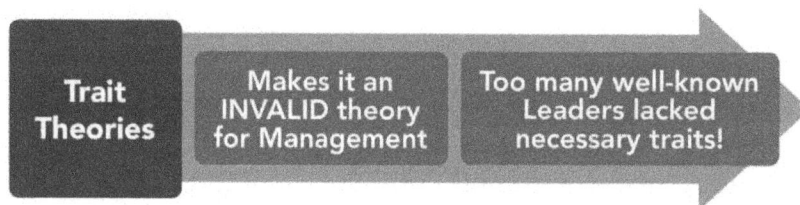

Trait Theories

Makes it an INVALID theory for Management

Too many well-known Leaders lacked necessary traits!

The need for effective leaders within organizations has led to theories and methodologies that rely on behaviours that can be learned rather than 'traits' that a person either does or does not have. This plethora of research has led to four different types of leadership theories.

- **Contingency theories**—say there is no one leadership style that suits all situations. Success comes from several factors of which leadership is one. Features of the situation and the followers are also significant.
- **Situational theories**—suggest that it is the circumstances that face a leader that determine their behaviour. Whether they alone or along with others share the knowledge needed to succeed.
- **Transactional or Exchange theories**—feature a defined transaction being made between a leader and his/her followers. Action is required when performance is above or below this agreed level.
- **Transformational theories**—concentrate on the links formed between a leader and his/her followers. This leader will inspire and motivate each team member to maximize their performance because they understanding the significance of the task overall.

Key Points

- ✓ Early leadership theories tend to focus on the character and personality of successful leaders, whilst later theories concentrate on what leaders actually do.
- ✓ Trait theories do not stand up to scrutiny even in the context of political or military leadership.
- ✓ There are four major types of leadership that have been identified and refined into more detailed leadership models.
- ✓ Knowledge of these models can help you to become a better leader by providing insight into your own leadership behaviours.

Ten Leadership Theories

A working knowledge of these is essential if you want to become a successful leader because each one can offer you valuable insight into your own behaviour. This eBook describes ten of the most popular leadership theories.

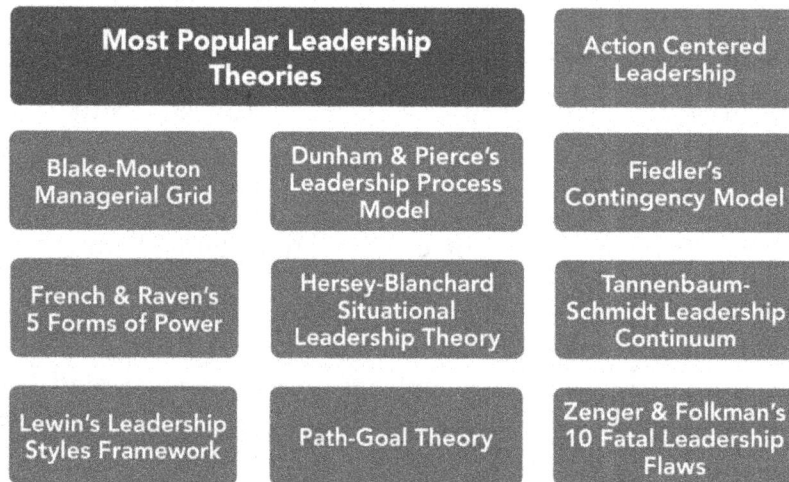

Most Popular Leadership Theories		Action Centered Leadership
Blake-Mouton Managerial Grid	Dunham & Pierce's Leadership Process Model	Fiedler's Contingency Model
French & Raven's 5 Forms of Power	Hersey-Blanchard Situational Leadership Theory	Tannenbaum-Schmidt Leadership Continuum
Lewin's Leadership Styles Framework	Path-Goal Theory	Zenger & Folkman's 10 Fatal Leadership Flaws

One of the great challenges when it comes to proper leadership is balancing the various interests of those who you are required to lead. Not everyone is going to have the same goals and aspirations, even within the same business or organization.

Therefore, it is the job of a good leader to reconcile all of those various interests and bring them together in a way that keeps the team working in the right direction. With good leadership, it is possible to bring everyone together in a common pursuit even if they have divergent goals among themselves.

Action Centred Leadership

The Action Centred Leadership (ACL) model presented by John Adair back in 1973 is notable because it can help reconcile the various goals and desires of individuals. While still accomplishing the specific goals set out for the team and the project as a whole.

At its simplest form, the model can be described by how it divides leadership into the areas of 'Task', 'Team' and 'Individual'. Each element plays an important role in the leadership picture, and only when all three are balanced properly will the leader be achieving success.

Harmony among the three might not always be the easiest goal to reach, but it is the job of the leader to make it happen. Looking at each element in turn you can understand how each of these three aspects is important.

It All Starts with a Task

Without a task, there is no reason to have a team made up of individuals, and no reason to lead them in the first place. Every leadership role is developed because there is a goal in mind, and someone needs to be in charge of directing the team toward that goal. Such a goal can be rather general, such as simply running a profitable business, while other goals will be very specific — like developing a new product to launch to market by the end of the year. No matter what the goal is, that task is what will guide the leadership that has to be provided to the team.

The Task guides the leadership style needed to accomplish it.

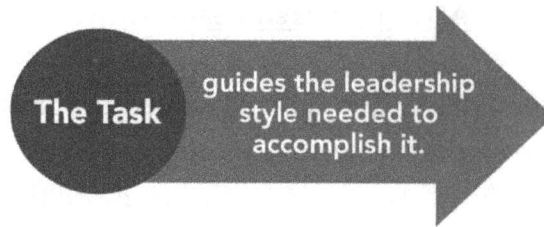

Speaking of the variety of tasks that are possible for a leader to work toward, one of the most important jobs of the leader is to actually define and identify the task at hand. Sometimes this will be quite easy, but other times it can actually be a serious challenge. Teams work together better when they are clear on the task at hand, so providing that definition in no uncertain terms is a major part of the equation.

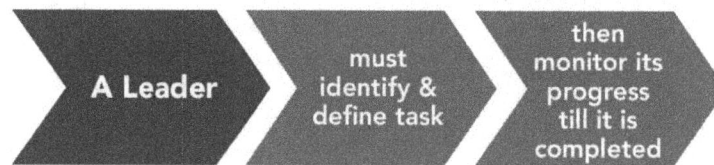

A Leader must identify & define task then monitor its progress till it is completed

Among the other important parts of the task including identifying milestones along the way that need to be met, establishing who is responsible for which part of the task, and what will be defined as success in the end. Monitoring progress and making sure that the group is getting closer and closer to accomplishing the task falls on the leader, and is an important part of the Action Centred Leadership model.

Teamwork is Essential

Leading the team is what most people think of traditionally as being 'leadership'. Any given team is made up of individuals with various skills and experiences, so it is up to the leader to extract the best possible performance from each of them. The leader should define how the team works together, such as communication standards and methods for resolving conflict. Whenever two or more people are working together on a task there is bound to be conflict along the way — the best leaders are able to moderate those conflicts and resolve them quickly.

Encouragement is another important part of the Action Centered Leadership plan, especially for long projects. The members of the team need to remain focused on the 'prize' at the end of the task so they can remain motivated and determined to reach a successful conclusion to the project. Making sure that the team as a whole feels invested in the success of the group is something that a good leader will be able to accomplish

Don't Forget About the Individuals

Forgetting about individuals within the team is probably the most common leadership mistake that is made by managers in all areas of business. It is tempting to just treat each individual as a robot who is programmed to only do what is best for the organization—but real life is just not that simple. Individual people have varying desires, fears, experiences, motivations, etc.

Extracting the best from each person on the team means treating them as the individual that they are. Offering rewards or praise for a strong contribution to the team is a common tact for getting the best possible performance from members of the team. Only when the leader is able to place each person in the role that is best suited for their skills and interests will the team be able to function as successfully as possible.

Action Centred Leadership is a popular leadership model to follow in large part because of the simplicity that it offers. Just by understanding the basics of the three areas of leadership provided in this model—Task, Team, and Individual—a leader will be well on the way to a successful project. Each of these three areas is vitally important, and it will be difficult to succeed in one area without support from the other. Bringing all three together properly isn't always going to be easy, but it is a goal that each leader in an
organization should strive to achieve.

Key Points

- ✓ Action cantered leadership involves balancing task, team and individual focus.
- ✓ Each of these three elements plays an important role in the leadership picture, and only when all three are balanced properly will the leader be achieving success.
- ✓ No matter what the goal is, that task is what will guide the leadership that has to be provided to the team.

✓ Making sure that the team as a whole feels invested in the success of the group is something that a good leader will be able to accomplish.

✓ Only when the leader is able to place each person in the role that is best suited for their skills and interests will the team be able to function as successfully as possible.

Blake-Mouton Managerial Grid

It's no secret that there are a variety of different management and leadership styles out there. In fact, you could argue that there is a different managerial style for each individual person that serves in a leadership role.

The Blake-Mouton Managerial Grid is a system that can be used to group like leaders into categories based on the methods that they use.

While no organizational system will ever be perfectly complete, this grid is a great way to understand more about certain leadership styles and how they work. Dating back to the early 1960's, this is a framework that has stood the test of time and remains relevant today.

The two dimensions of this grid quickly identify the priorities of the manager in question— 'Concern for People' and 'Concern for Results'. It doesn't get much simpler than that, and it shouldn't take long to determine where along this grid you fit as a leader.

- Concern for People. The leader that emphasizes Concern for People over Results is one who is trying to do their best to further the careers of those they are leading. As the decisions are being made regarding who will work on what parts of a project. For example this leader is thinking before making assignments:

    o Which tasks will help each individual progress their careers?
    o Which tasks are likely to be enjoyed?

- Concern for Results. Naturally, this is the opposite of the previous approach. With this kind of leadership, the only concern is for the job getting done as successfully as possible. This leader is one who sets aside any level of focus on the individuals and only things about the bigger picture for the organization. Whatever tasks need to be assigned to specific people in order to get the job done right is what will be done. If the individuals within the group don't like it, that will be their problem to deal with.

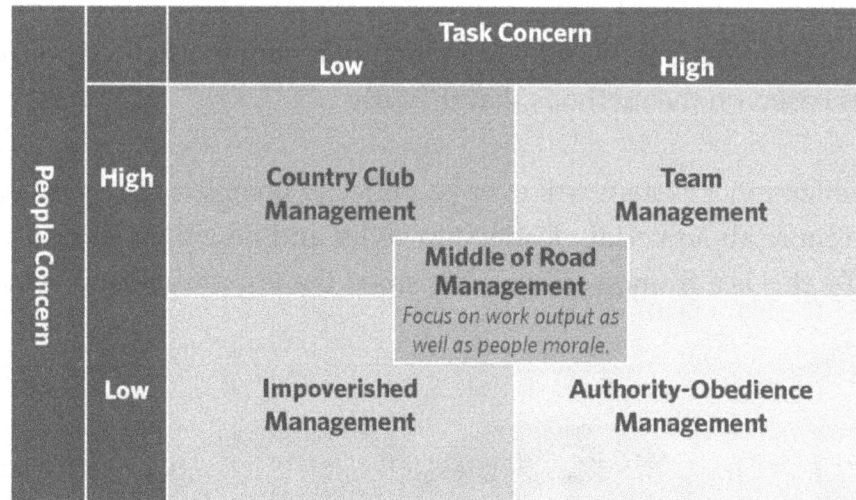

		Task Concern	
		Low	High
People Concern	High	Country Club Management	Team Management
		Middle of Road Management *Focus on work output as well as people morale.*	
	Low	Impoverished Management	Authority-Obedience Management

The real benefit of using the Blake-Mouton Managerial Grid comes when you start to look at it in terms of four quadrants, and what each of those means for the manager. When plotted on the grid based on the two dimensions, there are four possible quadrants that a management style.

- **Impoverished Management** — in this case, the manager is failing both in terms of the task and the people and is not a desirable position. The work isn't being completed successfully enough to satisfy the needs of the organization, and the individuals involved aren't getting what they need out of it either.

  This is a systemic failure, and will usually result in bad outcomes for the leader in question. Getting out of this quadrant as soon as possible should always be the goal of a manager who finds that they are failing on both fronts.

- **Country Club Management** — most employees will love their manager when this kind of system exists. The results may be suffering, and the manager's superiors may not be impressed with their performance, but the employees are happy because they are being put first and having their needs met through the actions of the leader.

While the short-term results of this method may be enjoyable because the work environment is free of tension and conflict, the long-term results tend to be less beneficial once the results come in and the group is falling short of expectations.

- **Authority-Compliance Management** — is the opposite of the Country Club management position. Instead of paying sole attention to the employees, this lead is only serving the needs of the project and the results they are looking for.

  While they might reach the end goal, bridges could be burned in the meantime through the methods that are used. Unhappy employees tend to leave sooner, or decrease in production as their attitude drops. Short-term projects may benefit from this kind of strict management style, but it is unlikely to succeed over time.

- **Team Management** — offers the best of both worlds. This manager is able to successfully juggle the needs of the organization as a whole with the needs of the individual employees involved.

  Of course, since this is the best model for most managers to strive for, it is also the most difficult to achieve. The needs of your employees might not always correlate with what the company is looking for, so getting those things to balance out and keep everyone happy is a battle that takes time and effort to win.

  However, it will be worth the effort because the leader who is able to reach this quadrant of the grid is one that is likely to be well-received by his or her superiors for their work.

In the real world, things aren't always as black and white as they can appear on a grid and managers often adopt the 'Middle of the Road' management approach. This means sometimes the focus is concentrated more on the task and at other times more on the people. Leadership styles and decisions take on many different shapes, and it isn't always easy to decide how they fit into a certain mould.

The Blake-Mouton Managerial Grid is a good starting point for understanding the basic leadership options that a manager has when dealing with their employees. Avoiding the extremes and trying to balance all of the various interests at any one time is usually the best tact to take. Whether using the grid to evaluate yourself or someone else in your organization, it is a tool that remains useful decades after its creation.

Key Points

- ✓ The Blake-Mouton Managerial Grid is a system that can be used to group like leaders into categories based on the methods that they use.
- ✓ It uses a two dimensional grid to identify the priorities of the manager in question.
- ✓ The axes are 'Concern for People' and 'Concern for Results'giving four possible quadrants that a management style can land in.
- ✓ Impoverished Management—the manager is failing both in terms of the task and the people.
- ✓ Country Club Management—employees are happy because they are being put first and having their needs met through the actions of the leader.
- ✓ Authority-Compliance Management—the manager is focusing too much on getting the task done at the expense of their team's wellbeing.
- ✓ Team Management—the manager is able to successfully juggle the needs of the organization as a whole with the needs of the individual employees involved.

Dunham & Pierce's Leadership Process Model

The Dunham and Pierce Leadership Process Model doesn't necessarily seek to define leadership, but it does the job indirectly. This model addresses all of the key elements that play a role in leadership, and helps the manager to understand how each part affects the other parts of the equation.

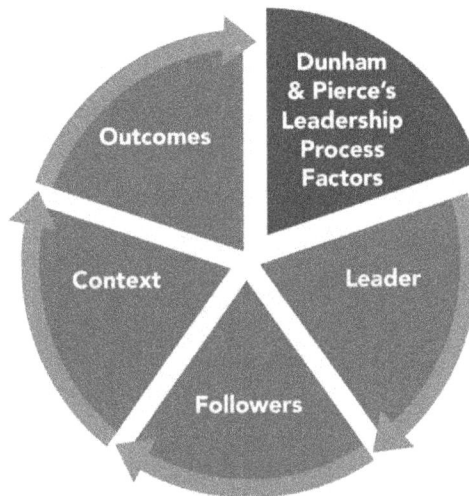

Leadership will never be simple, but using this model is a good way to 'get your head around' the various moving parts and hopefully bring it into better focus in your mind. According to Dunham and Pierce, there are four factors that play a role in the leadership process.

1. **Leader** — the person in charge of a project or team, regardless of what their title may be. That person may be referred to as an owner, a manager, a V.P., or any other title that confers power and responsibility. The important thing is that they are the person who a group of others answer to, and it is their performance that we are worried about with this model.

2. **Followers** — the people who are being led. Generally, these will be employees of the company in question. Most commonly, the Followers for a specific manager fall within a group or division of the company. The performance that the Leader is able to coax out of the Followers will largely be responsible for the outcomes that are achieved.

3. **Context** — refers to the circumstances under which the Leader is managing his or her team. Whether it is a project that will run for a predetermined length of time, or simply employees working on a day-to-day basis, the context of leadership plays an important part in what style of management is going to be most successful. This is an element that is often skipped over in some leadership models and discussions.

4. **Outcomes** — the results of any project or task that has been worked on by the Followers under direction of the Leader. For example, if a well-defined project has been worked on for two months, the success or failure of that project will be considered an Outcome. Above all else, leaders tend to be judged on their Outcomes because they usually have the most direct influence over the bottom line. If you are a manager within an organization, it is probably your Outcomes that you spend most of your time concerned with.

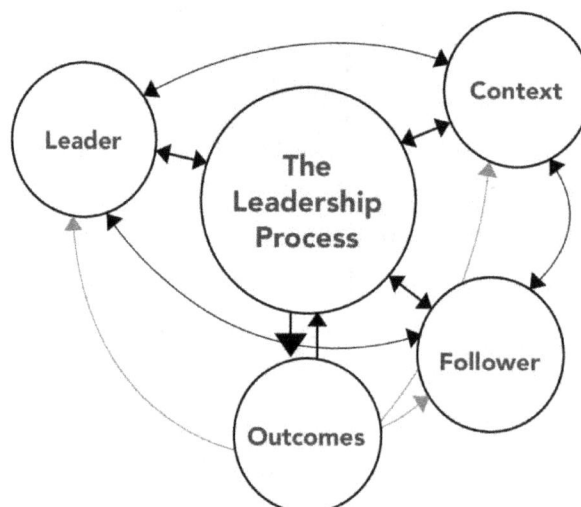

The overreaching theme of this model you should take away, it is that all of the aspects of leadership are interconnected in one way or another by a circular rather than linear relationship.

Your actions as the Leader will affect your followers
+
Your Followers actions are likely to affect you as a Leader (& your management style)
+
Learn from your team and how their actions dictate the Context and the Outcomes
=
A better chance of success.

So what does this have to do with management from a practical sense? It should serve as notice that everything done within the context of a leadership situation is important, and it all comes around in the end in one form or another.

Things that are done to help the team and empower the individuals on a team can serve to improve future outcomes, while any negativity is likely to manifest in unwanted ways. Taking a holistic approach to management can be powerful when it comes to guiding a team toward long-term success.

This model has plenty to teach leaders and managers in a variety of settings, but some of the most important lessons are:

- Grow relationships within the team. Since this model of leadership is circular in nature, it only makes sense that growing relationships well help everyone perform better. When the relationships are strong from the top down, communication will benefit and the team should work more efficiently as a whole.

- Let people do what they do best. This is key for any leader, no matter what context they are working in. When people are able to spend time working on projects that they feel comfortable with and that match up with their skill sets, they tend to be happier (and perform better). When leaders fail to consider the skills of their people, it should be no surprise the results lag.

- Offer feedback. This point goes along with the point regarding relationships among the team. Feedback is valuable because it helps to steer the members of the team in the right direction, in a positive way. Opening the lines of feedback helps the Followers learn what is expected from them, and also gives them an opportunity to provide feedback to the Leader—which can be invaluable.

- Act Ethically and Honestly. The circular nature of leadership dictates that it is vitally important to act with a high degree of honesty on a regular basis. When deceit creeps into the system, it is likely to spread and have a negative effect throughout the organization.

Leadership is complicated and sometimes scattered and chaotic, but the Dunham Pierce Leadership Process Model does a good job of highlighting the key points and identifying how they all affect one another. For the leader who is trying to keep a variety of different interests happy throughout the term of a project, this model can help to sort things out and keep them moving in the right direction.

Key Points

- ✓ The Dunham and Pierce Leadership Process Model addresses all of the key elements that play a role in leadership, and helps the manager to understand how each part affects the other parts of the equation.
- ✓ This model states that there are four factors that play a role in the leadership process: the Leader, the Followers, the Context, and the Outcomes.
- ✓ The meaning of Leader and Followers is self-evident. Context refers to the circumstances under which the Leader is managing his or her team and Outcomes refers to the results of any project or task that has been worked on by the Followers under direction of the Leader.
- ✓ The model suggests that everything done within the context of a leadership situation is important and if you are able to learn from your team and how their actions dictate the Context and the Outcomes, everyone will have a better chance at success

Fiedler's Contingency Model

Developed back in the 1960's by Fred Fiedler, Fiedler's Contingency Model is an interesting look at leadership styles and how different approaches can lead to very different results depending on the circumstances. As the term 'contingency' would indicate, this model is based on the idea that rather than having a single leadership style for all circumstances, the best approach is to be able to vary the leadership that is provided based on the group and task at hand.

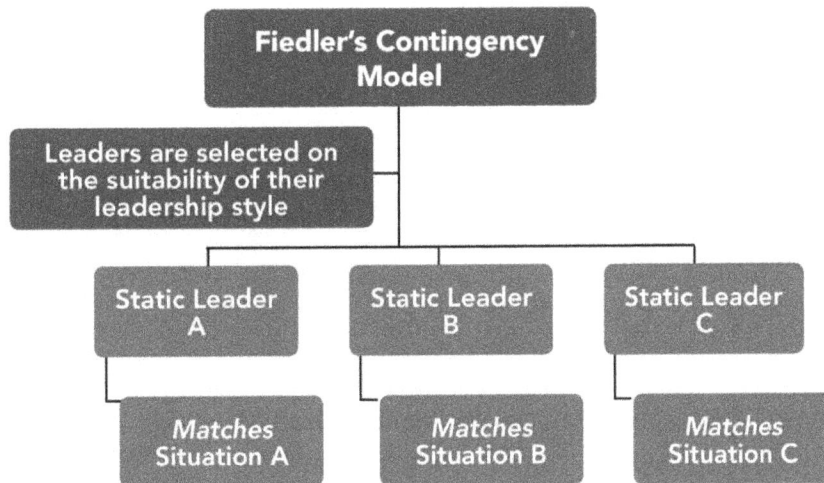

Fielder argues in this model that a specific leader is only able to lead in one fashion, meaning that another person will need to be tasked with the job if a different leadership style is required.

Right away, there are some elements of this model that make sense when you think about how they will be applied. Most people would agree that a 'one size fits all' approach is not going to be effective when it comes to leadership—rather, it will take a variety of styles and techniques to achieve success in the long run. However, the idea that an individual leader is unable to change their ways based on the needs of their team is one that will likely be argued by many. Regardless of where you stand on this topic, the model is certainly worth taking a closer look at for its many interesting insights.

Starting with the idea of a leader who is unable to change his or her ways, referred to as a 'Static Leader'. Fiedler uses a scale to determine what kind of leader an individual will be (or already is). The scale used is the 'Least-Preferred Co-Worker' scale and is the subject of much debate as to its practicality. Basically, this scale asks a series of questions that the leader is supposed to answer while thinking about their 'least favourite person that they have worked with over the years.

In order to arrive at a result, the leader is supposed to rank that person on a scale of 1-8 on a variety of personality traits such as Unfriendly to Friendly, and Hostile to Supportive. There are 16 of these rankings to complete, after which the leader will be left with a score that they can use to identify where they fall within the leadership spectrum.

- Low scores show a leader is more focused on tasks as opposed to relationships.
- High scores represent a leader that is more focused on building relationships with their teams.

The idea that these numbers are 'set in stone' is something that many people will disagree with. It seems logical that leaders will develop and evolve over time, potentially changing the score that they would receive on this scale. Also, depending on the person in question whom they were thinking about while answering the questions, the results could be skewed based on one strongly negative memory.

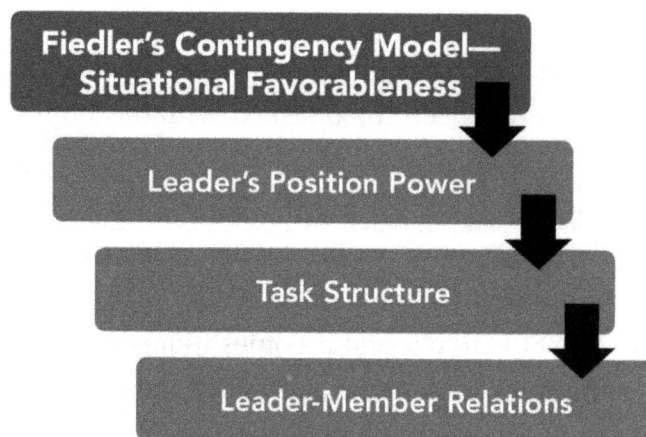

Making up the other half of this leadership model is the idea of 'Situational Favourableness'. Each of its three factors has a say in how a certain type of leader will fare in a given situation.

- Leader's Position Power. How much power is the leader being given in a situation? Is their word final when disputes arise, or does the next level of management dictate decisions down to the leader? The model classifies these rankings into two categories:

- o Strong leader one who has a high level of power within the organization.
- o Weak leader someone controlled from above to a greater degree.

- Task Structure. There are two kinds of tasks according to this model:

  - o Structured tasks are detailed and clear as to what they expect from each of the team members.
  - o Unstructured tasks may be open ended or undefined in terms of the goals and missions for the team.

- Leader-Member Relations. Judges how good the relationship is between the team members and the leader? The type of project that is being undertaken, and the ranking on the other two points on the Situational Favourableness scale will determine what kind of leader it takes to match up with the job. While most of the time a stronger relationship between leader and team is going to be preferred, that will not always be the case.

While Fiedler's Contingency Model is an interesting look at leadership styles and their effectiveness in certain situations, the limitations are pretty evident right from the start. Basing a person's leadership style on their interactions with one single co-worker could potentially lead to a misleading outcome, and each of the three factors probably aren't as black and white as they are required to be in order to use this model.

However, using this model to get an idea of what kind of leadership style you use, and what circumstances will be best-suited for you to manage, is an opportunity to gain insight and perspective. The Contingency Model can help you think about how you manage, and why you might be more successful in some situations than in others.

Key Points

- ✓ Fiedler's Contingency Model is based on the idea that rather than having a single leadership style for all circumstances, the best approach is to be able to vary the leadership that is provided based on the group and task at hand.
- ✓ Starting with the idea of a leader who is unable to change his or her ways, we see that Fiedler uses a scale to determine what kind of leader an individual will be.
- ✓ Making up the other half of this leadership model is the idea of 'Situational Favorableness', which has three components: Leader's Position Power, Task Structure, and Leader-Member Relations.
- ✓ Leader's Position Power refers to how much power is the leader being given in a situation. A strong leader is one who has a high level of power within the organization, while a weak leader is controlled from above to a greater degree.
- ✓ Task Structure—structured tasks are detailed and clear as to what is expected from each of the team members, whereas unstructured tasks may be open ended or undefined in terms of the goals and missions for the team.
- ✓ Leader-Member Relations refers to the relationship between the team members and the leader.
- ✓ Fiedler's Contingency Model can give you some insight into the leadership styles available to you provided that you are aware of its limitations.

French & Raven's Five Forms of Power

What is the difference between leadership and power? The answer to that question might not be quite as easy at is seems at first. In fact, the more you think about it, the more you likely come to the realization that leadership and power might be the same thing.

In any situation where one person is deemed to be the 'leader', they are likely also the person with the most power to make decisions. If you find yourself in a position of leadership within your organization, it is safe to say that you have a good deal of power as well.

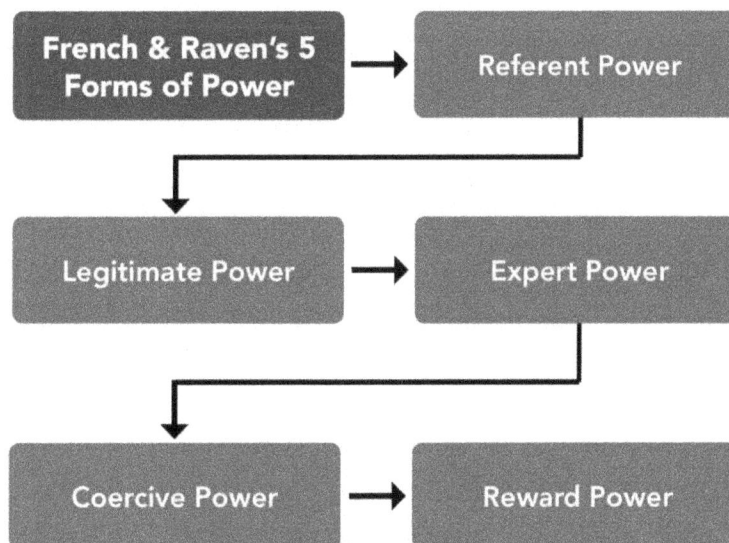

The 'Five Forms of Power' research was conducted by John French and Bertram Raven in 1959 and was important because it strived to determine what it is that makes someone powerful in a given setting. By describing each of the five types of power, you can assess your leadership capabilities.

1. **Reward Power**—is one of the more common types of power. The 'reward' can take many different forms, but it is typically financial when talking about a leader within a company. If you have the ability to reward your team members with things like bonuses or raises, you have the ability to command their attention through those rewards. Assuming the team members you lead are

interested in achieving the rewards that you can offer, they will be likely to work well with you in order to improve their chances of receiving the rewards.

One of the problems that can arise from using rewards to command power is when you aren't able to offer rewards that are appealing to those whom you lead.
For example,

If you don't have the power in your company to offer financial rewards of any significance, you have to try to appeal to your team with other benefits and perks that might not be as desirable to them.

In order for reward leadership to be effective, the leader must be able to offer rewards that the team members are striving to receive.

2. **Expert Power** — is achieved when you find yourself in a position of expertise based on your knowledge or experience. For example,

If you are working on a project with a group of co-workers whom are normally your peers — but you happen to be an expert in the specific field that you are dealing with — you may find yourself elevated to a position of authority and power.

However, often times this type of power is informal rather than official. You might find that you are commanding more attention in meetings and your opinion is being given more weight, but you might not have received any of the other typical signs of leadership.

Coming into power through being an expert in your field is something that can have long lasting benefits for your career. Because this kind of power is more organic than others — such as reward power — it is more likely to remain long after a specific project or task is completed. When others know that you are an authority on a given subject, that reputation should follow you throughout your career.

3. **Legitimate or Title Power** — is often the most recognized form of power and leadership, because it comes along with being appointed to a specific position. Why does the President have power? Because he holds the title of President, and

all of the authority that comes with it. In this case, the power is granted more because of a person's title than the individuals character.

Within organizations legitimate power tends to fall with the people who hold titles like Owner, CEO, Executive, and other similar positions. This kind of power can be extremely useful while it is held, but it tends to go away as soon as the title is taken back and given to someone else.

4. **Coercive Power**—leaders control their team members by the ability to take things away, rather than 'reward'. If you can fire someone based on their lack of performance on the team, for example, you have coercive power to influence their actions. They are likely to try to impress you and meet your expectations in order to keep their job.

   In many cases, coercive power is only good enough to get people to do the minimum required to avoid punishment. Unlike reward power, where team members may strive for excellence in order to achieve certain rewards, coercive leaders are more likely to get the bare minimum from their team who is simply hoping to stay out of trouble.

5. **Referent Power**—can be compared to an 'x-factor', because it is power that does not come for any obvious reason. Frequently, those who have referent power are simply well-liked by others based on their attitude, charm, or even good looks. They don't necessarily have any logical reason for having come to power, yet they still hold sway over many people for some reason. If you are naturally a person that others gravitate towards and want to talk to, there is a good chance you already have a measure of referent power.

Understanding what kind of power you have as a leader—and why you have it—is a valuable lesson that can be used to better lead people. Most likely, you will have some combination of the five types of power that are outlined above. Think about what kind of power you already have in your position, and what kind of power you should be working toward achieving to further your career.

Key Points

- ✓ French and Raven's Five Forms of Power attempts to determine what it is that makes someone powerful in a given setting.
- ✓ Reward Power is typically financial when talking about a leader within a company, for example the ability to reward your team members with things like bonuses or pay raises.
- ✓ Expert Power is achieved when someone finds themselves in a position of power based on their knowledge or experience.
- ✓ Legitimate Power can also be referred to a 'title power', because it is the power that comes along with being appointed to a specific position.
- ✓ Coercive Power is the opposite of reward power and is based on the ability to take things away. In the workplace this would normally mean being able to demote or fire someone.
- ✓ Referent Power is power that is not achieved by any of the above, and may be based on something intangible like popularity, attitude, or charm.
- ✓ This model can help you to understand what kind of power you already have, and what kind of power you should be working toward achieving if you want to further your career.

Hersey-Blanchard Situational Leadership Theory

Right in the name of this leadership theory, you can get a great indication of what it is all about. The term 'situational' indicates that:

Leaders should vary their approach based on the people they are leading, and the circumstances that surround the task at hand.

Indeed, the Hersey-Blanchard Situational Leadership Theory is one that is based around variable leadership, depending on a variety of circumstances. When a leader is able to adapt to the situation as quickly as possible, everyone will benefit in the end.

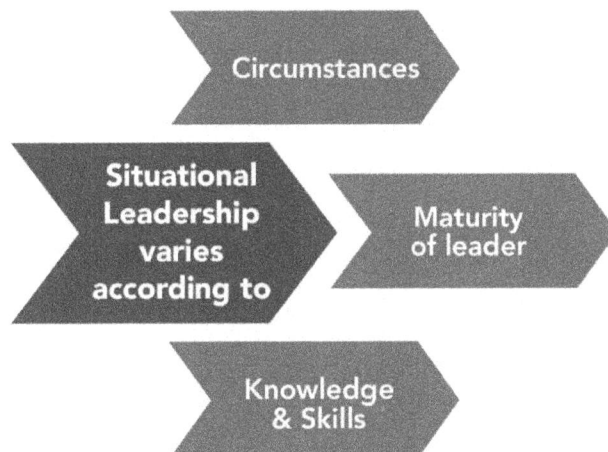

Specifically, this theory has to do with the maturity of those who are being led. To those who have worked as leaders in the past, it is no surprise that maturity should be considered when working on finding the right leadership style. For example,

Someone who is inexperienced in their field will likely lack the skills or confidence to take on tasks that would be comfortable for a more experienced employee.

Only when a leader is able to mould their approach to the maturity and talent of those that make up the team will the overall performance be up to par.

The Situational Leadership Theory offers up four potential leadership styles, and then four maturity levels that define the members of a team. Let's quickly look at each of the four styles and levels that can then be paired up for optimal performance.

Hersey-Blanchard Situational Leadership Theory		
	Task Behaviors	
	Low	High
High	**Participating Style** **Shares Ideas** (Followers able, unwilling, not confident)	**Selling Style** **Explain Decisions** (Followers unable, willing, confident)
Low	**Delegating Style** **Turn over decisions** (Followers able, willing, confident)	**Telling Style** **Give Instructions** (Followers unable, unwilling, not confident)

Relationship Behaviors

The four leadership styles that are presented in this theory are:

- **Telling**—is the most direct form of leadership. The leader of the group simply tells each member what to do, and how they would like them to do it. This approach is less collaborative, and more directive in nature. There is very little working together between the leader and the team members, instead the leader simply provides specific instructions for the team members to follow through with.

- **Selling**—has a little more room for collaboration. While the team members are still directed by the leader, the leader is more likely to engage with the team members along the way. The 'Selling' title comes from the idea that the leader may need to convince some of the team members to follow his or her lead and do things in a specific way.

- **Participating**—is a process where the leader tries to build relationships with those on the team—really becoming part of the team. This is quite a departure from the Telling style, as the leader will blend in more fully with those who are working as part of the team. In fact, the leader might not even make all of the decisions in this style, perhaps deferring at certain points to members of the team with more experience or knowledge in a given area.

- **Delegating**—represents the leader passing on most of the responsibilities for a given project or task to various members of the team. This style is something that leaders of experienced teams will often use, since the employees that are being led may not need much in the way of direction at this point in their careers.

To go along with those four leadership styles, the Hersey Blanchard Situational Leadership Theory also provides four maturity levels that describe those who are making up the team.

- **Maturity Level 1 (M1)**—These are the least experienced of workers. At this point, they will need to be instructed on how to do just about everything that makes up the task they are responsible for. While this usually means a leader is dealing with younger and less experienced employees, it could also be that the employees simply don't have much knowledge or background in the task at hand for a specific project.
  This maturity level matches up with the Telling leadership style, as the employees at this point will require complete direction for almost every task.

- **Maturity Level 2 (M2)**—Moving up a step, these are still inexperienced people who possess only slightly more knowledge and skill than those at the M1 level. Maturity is not only a measure of the ability than an individual has to deal with a task, but their willingness to take on the task in the first place. M2 team members are those who are more eager to work on a job, even if they aren't yet ready to do it correctly without the help of the leader of the group.
  The Selling leadership style is the proper match when dealing with M2 level team members.

- **Maturity Level 3 (M3)**—Getting close to the top of the scale, this group would include employees who are excited to work on a job and have most of the skill they need to get it done right. While they might not be able to quite get all of the job done without some help, they can get most of the way their on their own.
  The Participating style is the one that matches with M3 individuals, because they don't need full direction and are more able to engage with the leader for positive collaboration.

- **Maturity Level 4 (M4)** — At the top of the scale, those that are rated as M4 are completely capable of handling a task — and they know that they can get the job done without the help of the leader.

  Delegating is the leadership style of choice at this point simply because there is no need to be more involved than that. The team members have confidence, and expect to work independently.

The Hersey Blanchard Situational Leadership Theory promotes flexible leaders that are able to match their style to the experience and ability of those they are leading. Most people would agree that a good leader is a flexible one, and this theory falls right in line with that manner of thinking.

Key Points

- ✓ The Hersey-Blanchard Situational Leadership Theory is one that is based around variable leadership, depending on a variety of circumstances.
- ✓ The four leadership styles that are presented in this theory are Telling, Selling, Participating, and Delegating.
- ✓ To go along with those four leadership styles, the Hersey Blanchard Situational Leadership Theory also provides four maturity levels that describe those who are making up the team.
  - o At a maturity level of M1, team members need to be instructed on how to do just about everything that makes up the task they are responsible for.
  - o At a maturity level of M2, team members are those who are more eager to work on a job, even if they aren't yet ready to do it correctly without the help of the leader of the group.
  - o At a maturity level of M3, team members might not be able to quite get all of the job done without some help, but they can get most of the way their on their own.
  - o At a maturity level of M4, team members are completely capable of handling a task and they know that they can get the job done without the help of the leader.
- ✓ The Hersey Blanchard Situational Leadership Theory promotes flexible leaders that are able to match their style to the experience and ability of those they are leading.

Tannenbaum-Schmidt Leadership Continuum

Many leadership models and theories like to lump leadership strategies into just two or three categories and analyze them from there. While this can be helpful to get a general picture of how leadership works and what styles work under which circumstances, real life is usually more complicated than that. For this reason, a continuum makes a lot of sense because it covers a wider range of actual leadership approaches.

The Tannenbaum-Schmidt Leadership Continuum is a great example of this line of thinking. The continuum runs the spectrum of potential styles, and leaves plenty of leeway to land somewhere in the middle of the spectrum. Rare is the leader who will find themselves completely on one end of the equation or the other—nearly everyone will fall somewhere in the middle depending on their experience, personality, and the tasks that they are leading.

Tannenbaum-Schmidt Leadership Continuum

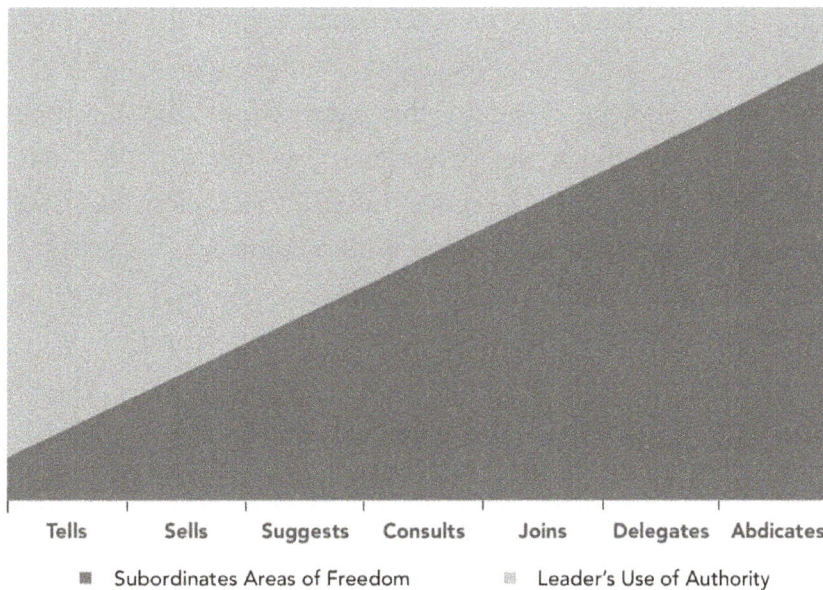

| Tells | Sells | Suggests | Consults | Joins | Delegates | Abdicates |

■ Subordinates Areas of Freedom   ▨ Leader's Use of Authority

Before getting into the details of the points along the continuum, it is important to understand the extremes that mark each end.

- **Manager-oriented Leadership** — means that the leader acts mostly like a dictator, telling the team members what to do and leaving very little (or no) room for negotiation.

  Most commonly, this is a strategy employed by leaders who are dealing with an inexperienced team, or a tight deadline that they have to meet. However, even the most strict leader will typically leave at least a little room for discussion and collaboration.

- **Team-oriented Leadership** — As you might imagine, this is a leader who provide his or her team with plenty of flexibility and encourages collaboration and the sharing of ideas.

  Usually, this sort of latitude will only be afforded to a team that has a high level of experience and acumen in a given area. This kind of leader must have a great deal of trust in their team to allow such freedom.

Within those extremes, the Tannenbaum-Schmidt Leadership Continuum highlights seven points along the way that can be used to describe various leadership styles.

- **Tells** — This style is very close to the extreme, as the team is given direct instructions and the interaction between the leader and the team members is very limited. Most of the time, a leader will use this style when they lack the trust that comes with experience in working with a team.

  As time passes and a team works together more and more, the leader will usually evolve away from this direct management method.

- **Sells** — Sliding a bit up the scale, this point is marked by leadership which is still direct, but also allows for a little bit of back and forth between the leader and the team. In the end, it is the leader that will be calling the shots, but at least the team is provided with the opportunity to give some input and have their voice be heard.

- **Suggests** — When a leader using a suggesting style, they are softer in their approach to the team and want to make sure that the team feels like they have real, valued input in the process. How much that input is actually taken into consideration will depend on the level of experience among the team, and how much trust the leader has in them at this point.

However, this style can go a long way toward growing the experience of the team as it allows them a little more insight into the process than the previous two styles on the list.

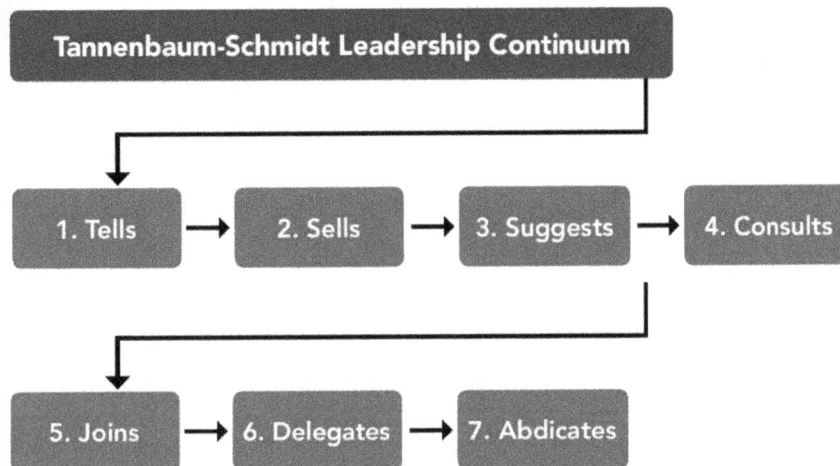

Tannenbaum-Schmidt Leadership Continuum

1. Tells → 2. Sells → 3. Suggests → 4. Consults

5. Joins → 6. Delegates → 7. Abdicates

- **Consults** — As the name would indicate, this style of leadership is increasingly collaborative between the leader and the team. A leader is only going to feel comfortable moving to this position on the continuum when they are sure that the team members are experienced enough to put trust in their thinking and decision making.
  This style goes beyond 'superficial' interaction with the team and actually gives them power over how the process is going to be dealt with. While consulting requires a team with experience and skill, it is a great way to keep all of the members of the team engaged in the process.

- **Joins** — At this point along the line, the leader starts to become more a member of the team than a dictator who is telling everyone what to do. While the leader retains the power in the situation and will be the one responsible for making choices in the end, the team is genuinely used to help make decisions.
  This kind of leadership is usually the choice of someone who is leading an experienced team made up of individuals who have highly developed skills in their specifics areas of expertise.

- **Delegates** — Moving closer to the other extreme, the leader who delegates is one who has a high degree of trust in his or her team. Rather than becoming a part of the team, the leader 'steps back' from the team and trusts them to get the job done.

Usually, there will be parameters put in place to make sure the team stays on track and is working toward the right goal, but the leader isn't necessarily involved in the day-to-day decision making process.

- 7-**Abdicates** — is at the other end of the spectrum. It represents a point where the leader essentially relinquishes any involvement and trust the team to get the job done from start to finish.

The only connection the leader has to the team is bearing responsibility for the work that they do.

It is obvious that trust and experience are going to be essential to success at this end of the leadership continuum.

Using the Tannenbaum-Schmidt Leadership Continuum is an excellent way to understand the various approaches that leaders can take to managing their teams. Since it is more nuanced than many other leadership theories, a wider variety of leaders will find this tool to be a useful one. As you prepare to lead a new team, or work on improving the performance of your current team, consider the various styles represented within this model.

Key Points

- ✓ The Tannenbaum-Schmidt Leadership Continuum describes a spectrum of leadership behaviors from autocratic to democratic.
- ✓ Within those extremes, it highlights seven points along the way that can be used to describe various leadership styles.
- ✓ The 'Tells' style involves the team being given direct instructions about how to accomplish the task.
- ✓ The 'Sells' style allows for a little bit of back and forth between the leader and the team is provided with the opportunity to give some input and have their voice heard.
- ✓ The 'Suggests' style is designed to make the team members feel like they have real, valued input into how the task is going to be accomplished.
- ✓ The 'Consults' style works when a leader is sure that the team members are experienced enough to put trust in their thinking and decision-making.

- ✓ The 'Joins' style involves the leader becoming more a member of the team than a dictator who is telling everyone what to do.
- ✓ The 'Delegates' style involves the leader stepping back from the team and trusting them to get the job done according to a predetermined brief.
- ✓ The 'Abdicates' style represents where the leader essentially relinquishes any involvement and trusts the team to get the job done from start to finish.

Lewin's Leadership Styles Framework

Not only can leadership strategies vary from person to person, but the same person can often use different strategies in different situations in order to achieve maximum results. The leader who is stuck in only one way of thinking and never responds to the changes going on around them is one who is unlikely to be a leader for long.

The Lewin's Leadership Styles Framework dates back many years—to the 1930's, in fact—but it is still relevant today because it divides leadership styles up into three easy to remember groups. While these groups might not necessarily capture all of the subtlety that is contained within a given leader or manager, they do a good job of highlighting the overall approach.

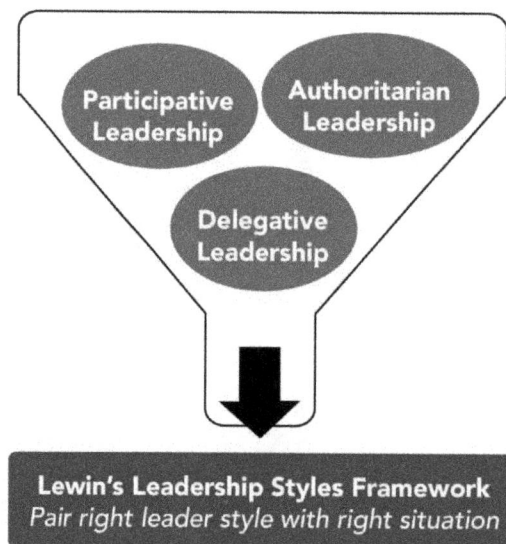

Based on the situation, any of these three styles could be the perfect one for the job. At the same time, any of these three could be the wrong one for the job if used under incorrect circumstances. Pairing the right leadership style with the right situation is a task that every leader should take quite seriously. The three leadership styles that Kurt Lewin presented in his framework are:

Authoritarian Leadership—This leader is one who takes command and doesn't care to pass on any of the decision-making responsibility to members of his or her team. An authoritarian leader makes decisions independently and is convinced that they are the correct decision for the circumstances regardless of the feelings of any members of the team. Typically, there would be very little interaction between the leader and team members under this type of leadership style.

The leader will pass down assignments and objectives to the team, with specific instructions on how to get the job done. There are both positives and negatives associated with this style of leadership.

- On the positive side, it can be an effective strategy when dealing with an inexperienced team who lacks the knowledge to take a more autonomous role in the project. When a team is made up of individuals who need specific instructions to succeed, the authoritarian leader could be the perfect choice for the job.
- At the same time, an experienced team might push back against this type of leadership because it doesn't offer them the freedom and creativity that they feel they have earned.

It is important that the leader evaluate carefully the members of the team before deciding how to best lead them through any task.

Participative Leadership—this type of a leader is going to get involved as part of the team and get to work. While they remain in charge and hold decision-making power, the process is far more collaborative and cooperative. Team members are encouraged to give their ideas and their feedback, for the good of the group as a whole.

The leader will consider ideas put forward by the team and may take them up if it is deemed to be in the best interest of the project. Generally speaking, this kind of leader is better-liked by the members of the team because they are seen as one of the group—as opposed to acting as a dictator who simply passes down orders.

Of course, this type of leadership will not work with every team. Thinking about the inexperienced team from the previous example, participative leadership might not be the right way to get them through a project.

- Without strong leadership, their lack of experience could become a major problem.

- However, a team with moderate experience and plenty of enthusiasm could be just right for this option. As long as there is enough knowledge in the group to keep the project moving in the right direction, the participation of the leader should only further the productivity achieved.
- Also, the members of the team may stay better engaged and motivated because they feel invested as part of the process.

Delegative Leadership — is the most 'hands off' from the leader's perspective. A leader who delegates the majority a project is one that has complete trust in his or her team and will allow them to run with the job. Other than monitoring the progress of a given project, and checking in the status of the work from time to time, this leader will likely leave the team members alone to do what they do best.

Not surprisingly, this is typically the preferred style of the leadership from the team member's perspective — having a leader who is available when needed, but not getting in the way or micromanaging the work. It should go without saying that using this management style with a team who isn't prepared to handle it properly is a recipe for disaster.

- An inexperienced team, or one that isn't properly motivated and focused on the task at hand, could use the freedom provided by leadership delegation to get off-task and fall behind on project deadlines.

If a leader is going to trust his or her reputation to the performance of the team, they need to be highly confident in each member of that group.

As you can see, the three styles of leadership put forward by Lewin's Leadership Styles Framework each can be successful when put to use in the right time and place. Trying to use the wrong style with the wrong group of people, however, could lead to big trouble for both the members of the team and the leader.

As the group evolves and changes over time, so too should the management style that is being used adapt to the needs of the team as a whole. When the leadership style closely matches the profile of the team in question, great results can occur.

Key Points

- ✓ Lewin's Leadership Styles Framework divides leadership styles up into three easy to remember groups.
    - o Authoritarian Leadership involves the leader passing down assignments and objectives to the team, with specific instructions on how to get the job done.
    - o Participative Leadership is collaborative and cooperative. Team members are encouraged to give their ideas and their feedback, for the good of the group as a whole.
    - o Delegative Leadership is the most 'hands off' from the leader's perspective and the leader needs to have complete trust in his or her team and be prepared to allow them to run with the job.
- ✓ The three styles of leadership put forward by Lewin's Leadership Styles Framework each can be successful when put to use in the right time and place.

Path-Goal Theory

Any time there is a leader being placed in charge of a team, it is a safe bet that there is a goal or an objective at stake. Whether than goal is short-term, such as creating a new product that will launch in three months, or longer term like developing a branding strategy over the next five years, the goal is out there to be reached. Without goals, teams would have no target to direct their activities and productivity would be almost impossible to achieve.

At the same time, there is a path that leads the way to those goals. It might help to think of the path as the day-to-day reality of the process that is needed to reach the goal. Inevitably there will be roadblocks along this path—some small, and some large—so team members will need to be creative and agile in order to get around the blocks and stay on course to reach the target.

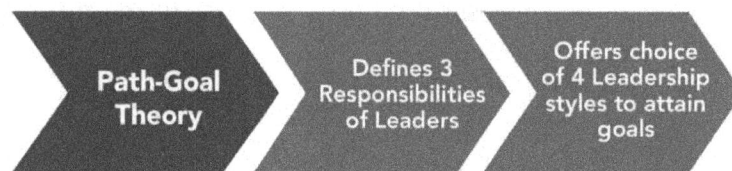

But what role does the leader play in this process? Trying to help a leader define their place in this equation so that they can give the team they manage the support they need without getting in the way.

Striking the right balance between supportive and intrusive is a difficult thing to do. That is what the Path-Goal Theory is all about and was developed by Robert House in the early '70's. He presented three different responsibilities that leaders take on throughout a project.

- ✓ **Clearing the path.** Basically, this refers to the process of helping see the way from the start to the finish. While the end goal might be clearly defined, the midpoints that need to be reached in order to arrive at the end successfully might be a little harder to identify. An experienced leader should be able to help his or her team figure out the best path to reach the goals that they are charged with. Frustration is quick to set in among team members when they can't figure out which direction to head, so taking command at this point of the process is a sign of strong leadership.

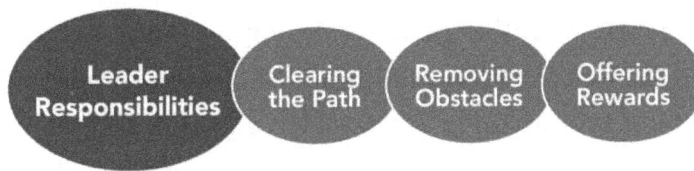

✓ **Removing obstacles**. Rare is the project that doesn't run into difficulties along the way. When the team is confronted with challenges that they aren't immediately able to resolve, the leader may need to step in and take control of the situation. This could be as simple as providing the team with resources that they need to solve a problem, such as adding a new team member that brings a specific skill to the group.

In order to make sure a project stays on schedule and is completed successfully, a leader will want to watch out for major roadblocks standing in the way of the team.

✓ **Offering rewards**. Motivation is a big part of success in any endeavor, but especially in ones that take place over long periods of time. Making sure that the individual members of the team are properly motivated and excited to work on the project is as important as anything else that takes place.

Whatever kind of motivation that a leader can offer—usually financial, but also including time off or other perks—can serve to maintain morale among the group and keep them charging ahead toward a successful conclusion.

In order to achieve those three objectives above, the Path-Goal Theory highlights four different styles of leadership that could be used. Naturally, it is up to the team leader to determine which of these styles—or what kind of blend—will be best to get the team from the start of the project to the finish.

- ✓ **Supportive leadership** — represents a setting in which the leader is working to build relationships with the individual people on the team. Showing an interest in each individual as a person is a highlight of this method, which is important in terms of keeping morale high. A supportive leader likely already knows that the team members are capable of getting the job done, so they focus their efforts instead of managing relationships.

- ✓ **Directive leadership** — is evident in situations where the leader acts more like a dictator in terms of simply passing out assignments and objectives. Normally this kind of leading is done when the members of the team lack the needed experience to work more autonomously. Instead, they must be guided by hand throughout the process, so the leader takes a more powerful role right from the start.

- ✓ **Participative leadership** — is where the leader treats the members of the team more as equals than as subordinates. The team members' will likely feel empowered by this approach and it should spur them on to stay motivate and strive for success throughout the project. Their opinions will be valued and listed to by the leader, who will act more as a member of the team than a dictator of the group.

- ✓ **Achievement-oriented leadership** — the leader lays out opportunities along the path for team members feel rewarded and their accomplishments recognized as they drive towards completion. This is really only a viable option when the team is made up of experienced workers who don't need any guidance or assistance in order to get the job done right. When a leader notices that morale and motivation are lagging in the group, this style might be just the right fix.

The Path-Goal Theory lays out a clear method for getting a team from the start of a project to the finish. With the three responsibilities understood, and the four different styles of leadership in hand, the manager can set to work making sure their team has everything they need to complete the objective as required.

Key Points

- ✓ This theory presents three different responsibilities that leaders take on throughout a project, including clearing the path, removing obstacles and offering rewards.
- ✓ Clearing the path refers to the process of helping the team to produce a roadmap for the project.
- ✓ Removing obstacles means that when the team is confronted with challenges that they aren't immediately able to resolve, the leader may need to step in and take control of the situation.
- ✓ Offering rewards involves making sure that the individual members of the team are properly motivated to work on the project.
- ✓ Path-Goal Theory highlights four different styles of leadership that could be used to achieve the above objectives.

Zenger & Folkman's 10 Fatal Leadership Flaws

Leaders have flaws. No matter how qualified an individual is to hold a position, or how prominent that position may be, they are a still a human being just like anyone else. With that said, a smart leader will look at him or herself critically and be able to determine where their flaws may lie. While perfection is likely an unattainable goal, consistent and steady improvement is not. Rather than choosing to ignore any flaws that they may have, the best leader is the one who is able to acknowledge and address their shortcomings.

With this thinking in mind, Zenger and Folkman's 10 Fatal Leadership Flaws take a close look at the most common flaws that plague leaders within even the biggest companies in the world. This study is a relatively young one, only having been published a few years ago. However, it has already garnered plenty of attention and is a valuable reference for anyone in a leadership position.

1. **Lack of energy and enthusiasm**—A leader should always been the one providing the energy to a project or a team—not the other way around. When the leader lacks the energy and excitement to motive the team that they are in charge of, the project is destined to fail right from the start. Not everyone is going to be a cheerleader, but all leaders should be properly motivated and driven to succeed.

2. **Accept their own mediocre performance**—Settling for just good enough is never the hallmark of a quality leader. By setting the bar as low as possible and then claiming victory when they step over it, this kind of leader won't be responsible

for taking the organization to new heights. In order to find real achievement, it is important the leadership doesn't settle for just so-so.

3. **Lack clear vision and direction** — A leader isn't really a leader if they don't have a direction and vision of their own — they are simply a follower of a higher-ranking leader. In order to take the reins of a project or a team and guide it to a favorable conclusion, a good leader will be able to bring their own vision to the table. This approach to leadership requires confidence and determination because the choices that are made might leave the leader open to criticism in the case of setbacks.

4. **Have poor judgment** — Making decisions and proper judgments is at the heart of being a good leader. The whole idea behind leadership is having someone available to make the hard choices that need to be made from time to time. A good leader will have a knack for making the right call — while a poor manager will fall short in this area. There is really no way to know how an individual will fare in terms of judgment until they are put into the fire and tested.

5. **Don't collaborate** — Just because someone is put in a position of leadership doesn't mean they should set out on their own and ignore the input of others. Smart leaders know that collaboration is an opportunity to gain valuable insight from other intelligent people and further the cause of the organization as a whole. Often it is leaders who are insecure in their own abilities that resist the collaborative efforts of others.

6. **Don't walk the talk** — This is one of the classic mistakes of leadership — not leading by example. When a leader sets out specific guidelines or expectations and then fails to live up to them, it will not look good to the rest of the team. Instead, the leader should be the first one in line to obey all of the conditions that have been put in place to dictate the actions of everyone on the team. Only when they are willing to play by their own rules will they be seen as having integrity.

7. **Resist new ideas** — Good ideas can come from anywhere, but some leaders are too stubborn or scared to take them if they don't come from inside their own head. Resisting good ideas that come from others is a typical mistake of a bad leader. It shouldn't matter where an idea came from as long as it is genuinely in the best interest of the team — and the organization as a whole.

8. **Don't learn from mistakes** — Mistakes are always opportunities to do better next time — if a leader is willing to see them as such. A poor leader is more likely to make excuses for their mistakes then they are to learn from them. Those who don't learn from the mistakes they have made are destined to repeat them again and again. The top leaders in any organization are likely the ones who accept their failures and grow so that they don't make the same mistake in the future.

9. **Lack interpersonal skills** — At its core, leadership is all about interpersonal skills. The way a leader interacts with those who are on the team — as well as others in the organization — will largely determine their success or failure in the long run. The leaders who are well liked and are able to connect with those around them will be far more likely to be viewed favorably. Among leaders with similar performance results, the ones who have the best interpersonal skills will almost always rise to the top.

10. **Fail to develop others** — The best leaders are more concerned with the growth of those on their team then they are their own development. When a leader is completely committed to make each member of the team the best that they can be, the overall good of the organization is served. Selfish leaders will typically be short for their positions as the performance of the team is going to suffer.

Zenger and Folkman's 10 Fatal Leadership Flaws should be required reading for anyone in a position of leadership. Many leaders are unable to accept their own flaws and acknowledge the fact that they make mistakes — but that is exactly what a great leader is willing to do. If you are in a leadership position, take the time to look inwardly and think about these ten points. When you spot any of them in your own performance, take the necessary steps to correct your leadership style and you will be better for the effort.

Key Points

✓ Zenger and Folkman's 10 Fatal Leadership Flaws take a close look at the most common leadership flaws and is designed to help leaders acknowledge and address their shortcomings.

✓ If you are in a leadership position, take the time to look inwardly and think about these ten points.

✓ If you spot any of them in your own performance, then take the necessary steps to correct your leadership style and you will be better for the effort

Summary

It is evident that there are plenty of different ways in which a leader can manage his or her employees or team members. No matter the setting, there are a variety of options available to the leader depending on what strategy they believe will pull the best possible performance out of their team.

No two people are exactly alike, and even those who try to follow the same methods will inevitably have their own unique style that they use in an attempt to get the job done. While there is room for individuality in leadership, it is also important that a leader knows what style they are using and how it affects the outcomes and the people that they lead.

This Book describes the different ideas and teachings about leadership as a source of inspiration. These provide managers with a broad base from which to form the style of leadership most suited to them personally and the situation they are asked to manage. This toolkit helps you to develop your own leadership style based on your own personality, the task at hand and the team that you are leading.

Preface

This eBook describes ten popular contemporary leadership models. You can use these as inspiration and a potential toolkit from which you can develop your own leadership style based on your own personality, the task at hand and the team that you are leading.

It describes following leadership models:

- Mintzberg's Management Roles
- Lencioni's Five Dysfunctions of a Team
- Birkinshaw's Four Dimensions of Management
- Waldroop and Butler's Six Problem Behaviors
- Cog's Ladder
- Leader-Member Exchange Model
- Team Roles
- Benne and Sheats' Group Roles
- Margerison-McCann Team Management Profile
- The JD-R Model

Introduction

This eBook describes the ten most popular contemporary leadership models. You can use these as inspiration and a potential toolkit from which you can develop your own leadership style based on your own personality, the task at hand and the team that you are leading.

1. **Mintzberg's Management Roles**
   These cover ten tasks and responsibilities that a manager may need to perform. These are divided up into three categories: interpersonal, informational, and decisional.Interpersonalrolesinclude:figurehead,leaderandliaison.Informational roles include: monitor, disseminator and spokesperson. Decisional roles include: entrepreneur, disturbance handler, resource allocator, and negotiator. Any given manager may be asked to complete a variety of tasks during a given day depending on what comes up and what problems need to be solved.

2. **The 'Dysfunctions of a Team'**
   This model by Patrick Lencioni addresses some of the common problems that are found within teams. People working together toward a common goal is bound to lead to issues simply because every individual brings slightly different goals, aspirations, skills, and more to the table. While that is the great strength of a team, its diversity, it can also be its biggest weakness. Simply by understanding that these issues could exist within your team, you will be better prepared to identify and correct them as quickly as possible.

3. **Birkinshaw's Four Dimensions of Management**
   This model highlights four dimensions that represent key management processes and practices. You can use it to help you to understand how best to manage the type of work that you're doing, and the values of your organization.

4. **Waldroop and Butler's Six Problem Behaviors**
   This model aims to help managers by identifying six of these 'problem behaviors' along with their traits. When you see any of these six starting to become present in members of your team, taking quick action is the best option before their behavior becomes a detriment to the group as a whole.

5. Cog's Ladder

This model suggests there are five steps necessary for a small group of people to be able to work efficiently together. These stages are the polite stage, the why we're here stage, the power stage, the cooperation stage and the esprit stage. It is similar to Tuckman's Stages, another stage model of groups. Tuckman recognised 4 stages of team development: "Forming," "Storming," "Norming," and "Performing."

6. The Leader-Member Exchange Theory

This model looks at how your own personal opinions could end up limiting the opportunities that an individual has to succeed under your leadership. It is not particularly helpful in describing the specific leader behaviors that promote high- quality relationships as it only implies generalities about the need for leaders to show trust, respect, openness, autonomy and discretion.

7. Belbin's Team Roles

When looking at any team, it is quickly apparent that each member of the team adopts their own role in order to best contribute and use their skills in a way that is beneficial to the goals of the team as a whole. These roles usually develop naturally over time, depending on the makeup of the team and the specific task at hand. A good manager will observe the roles that are being filled on the team, and step in when necessary to balance out the composition of the group.

8. Benne and Sheats' Group Roles

This model recognises 26 roles that are divided up into one of three categories task roles, personal roles, and social roles. These role definitions are useful for looking at specific behaviors that occur within a group and evaluating it's current function and needs. They also provide a guide for team member development, as the more positive behaviors each person can display, the better able the whole group will be to respond to the demands put on it.

9. The Margerison-McCann Team Management Profile

This is a tool that organizations can use to help classify their employees in regard to what type of team member they are or will be. Using a set of 60 questions, this profile establishes some baseline information about each member of the team so that they can be placed into a specific spot on the Team Management Wheel. The more sections of the wheel that can be filled up by the members of a single team, the more complete that team will be.

10. The Job Demands-Resources (JD-R) Model

This model states that when job demands are high and job resources/positives are low, then both stress and burnout increase. The effects of high job demands can be offset by increasing the positive aspects of the job. You can achieve this by identifying and promoting the job positives that act as a buffer between your team members and the demands of their roles. These can include: Mentoring or coaching, training and development, regular constructive feedback, and increased autonomy.

Mintzberg's Management Roles

The role of 'manager' sounds simple enough, but anyone who has ever served as a manager knows that it is far more complex than it might appear at first. Being a leader in any organization is a complicated and challenging task that can take on a variety of forms depending on the needs of the organization and the people that are being led. Any given manager may be asked to complete a variety of tasks during a given day depending on what comes up and what problems need to be solved.

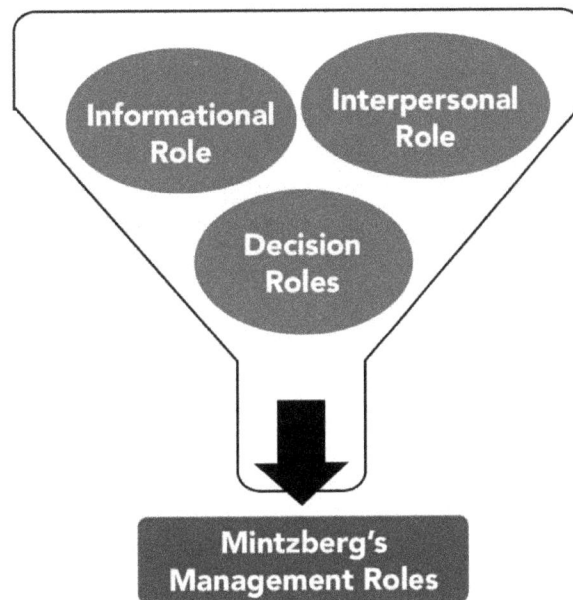

This is the general idea behind Mintzberg's Management Roles. These ten management roles were published as part of his book in 1990, and they cover the spectrum of tasks and responsibilities that a manager must take on at one point or another.

In order to better organize a long list of ten roles, they have been divided up into three categories—interpersonal, informational, and decisional. Below we will look at each of the ten roles, what they mean for the manager, and which of the three categories they fit into.

Figurehead

One of the important roles of a leader is simply to be a figurehead for the rest of the group. This is one of the interpersonal roles, because so much of it is about being someone that people can turn to when they need help, support, etc. A good leader will project confidence so that everyone involved feels a sense of security and reassurance that the job will be done right.

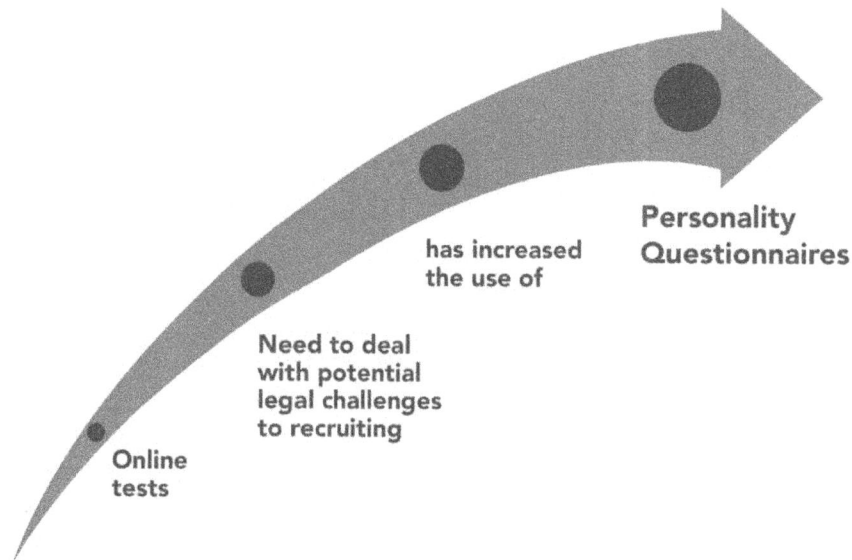

Online
tests

Need to deal
with potential
legal challenges
to recruiting

has increased
the use of

**Personality
Questionnaires**

Leader

Another interpersonal role, this one should be obvious. A manager needs to lead the people that he or she is in charge of guiding toward a specific goal. This can include telling them what to do and when to do it, organizing the structure of the team members to highlight specific skills that each possesses, and even offering rewards for a job well done.

Liaison

The final role within the interpersonal category, acting as a liaison means that the manager must successfully interface with a variety of people—both within the organization and on the outside—to keep things running smoothly. This point is all about communication, and it is one of the main things that determines the ultimate success or failure of a manager. Being able to properly communicate with a range of people in such a way that the project remains on track is a crucial skill to develop.

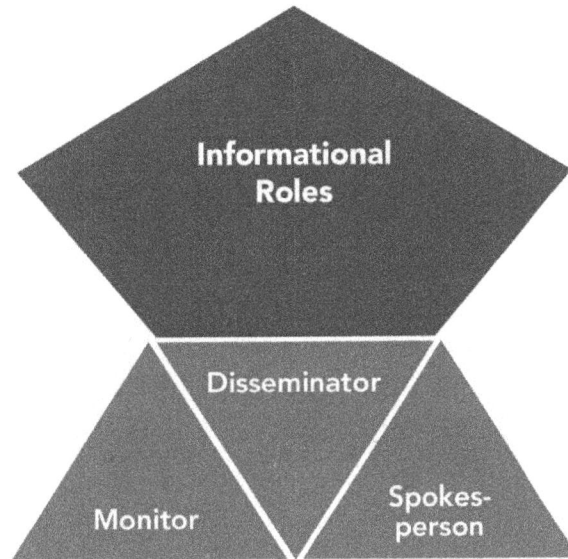

Monitor

Acting as a monitor is the first managerial role within the informational category. Just as the word would indicate, being a monitor involves tracking changes in the field that your organization works in, as well as changes on your team that might be signs of trouble down the road. Things are never static in business, so the successful manager is one who will constantly monitor the situation around them and make quick changes as necessary.

Disseminator

It does no good as a manager to collect information from a variety of internal and external sources if you are only going to keep it for yourself. The point of gathering that information is so that your team can benefit from it directly. So the next informational role is dissemination:

Getting information out quickly & effectively to the rest of your team.

Wasted time by the team members on a certain part of a project often has to do with them not possessing all of the relevant information, so make sure they have it as soon as possible.

Spokesperson

As the head of a team of any size or role within the organization, you will be the representative of that team when it comes to meetings, announcements, etc. Being a spokesperson is the final informational role on the list, and it is an important one because perception is often a big part of reality. Even if your team is doing great work, it might not be reflected as such to other decision makers in the organization if you aren't a good spokesperson.

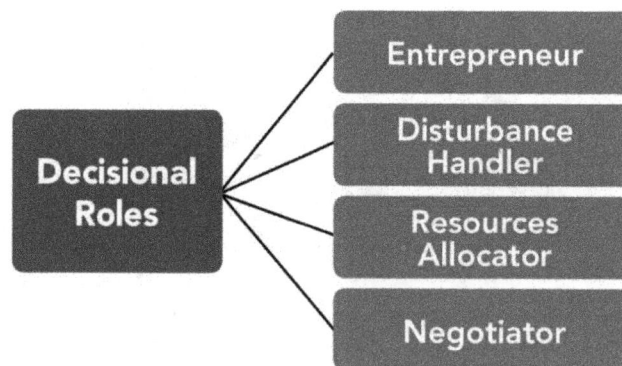

Entrepreneur

In some ways, being a manager within a larger organization is like running your own small business. While you will have managers above you to answer to, you still need to think like an entrepreneur in terms of quickly solving problems, thinking of new ideas that could move your team forward, and more. This is the first role within the decisional category on the list.

Disturbance Handler

It is almost inevitable that there will be disturbances along the way during any kind of project or task that involves more than one person. The second item in the decisional section of the list is being a disturbance handler, because getting back on track after a problem arises is important to short-term and long-term productivity.

Whether it is a conflict among team members or a bigger problem outside of the group, your ability to handle disturbances says a lot about your skills as a manager.

Resource Allocator

Every project is tackled using resources that are limited in some way or another. As a resource allocator, it is your job to best use what you have available in order to get the job done and meet your defined goals and objectives. Resources can include budget that has been made available for a project, raw materials, employees, and more. This is the third item within the decisional category, yet it is one of the most important things a manager must do.

Negotiator

Business is all about negotiation, and that is especially true for managers. The final role on the list, being a negotiator doesn't just mean going outside of the organization to negotiate the terms of a new deal. In fact, most of the important negotiation will take place right within your own team itself.

Getting everyone to buy in to the overall goal and vision for a project likely will mean negotiating with individual team members to get them to adopt a role that suits their skills and personal development goals. A good manager will be able to negotiate their way through these challenges and keep the project on track for success.

Key Points

- ✓ Mintzberg's Management Roles cover ten tasks and responsibilities that a manager may need to perform.
- ✓ These are divided up into three categories: interpersonal, informational, and decisional.
- ✓ Interpersonal roles include: figurehead, leader and liaison.
- ✓ Informational roles include: monitor, disseminator and spokesperson.
- ✓ Decisional roles include: entrepreneur, disturbance handler, resource allocator, and negotiator.
- ✓ Any given manager may be asked to complete a variety of tasks during a given day depending on what comes up and what problems need to be solved.

Lencioni's Five Dysfunctions of a Team

Whenever a team is constructed to work toward a goal, there are going to be problems. That isn't so much a negative statement as it is an honest one. If you are a manager who works in a leadership position in your organization, you know this to be true.

People working together toward a common goal is bound to lead to issues simply because every individual brings slightly different goals, aspirations, skills, and more to the table. While that is the great strength of a team—its diversity—it can also be its biggest weakness.

The 'Dysfunctions of a Team' book by Patrick Lencioni addresses some of the common problems that are found within teams. Anyone who has ever led a team, or even worked as part of a team, will likely be able to recognize each of these five problems. Simply by understanding that these issues could exist within your team, you will be better prepared to identify and correct them as quickly as possible.

Absence of Trust
The first dysfunction on the list is simply having team members who are unwilling to trust each other, or you as a leader. The natural tendency for many people is to want to be as self-reliant as possible, mostly because this is their job and they want to control

their own fate. Trusting a team member, or you as the leader, with part of their job feels risky because they could be seen in a bad light if things don't work out.

However, getting team members to trust each other is an important part of long-term success. It doesn't do much good to have assembled a team if that team is unwilling to support each and rely on each other to each tackle a small piece of the overall puzzle. Building trust is a challenge that every manager must face, but it is something that needs to be done in order to foster a successful and healthy team environment.

Fear of Conflict

Many people view conflict as always being a bad thing, when that isn't necessarily the case. While too much conflict is certainly bad within a team, a healthy amount of debate and discussion can lead to the best possible outcomes. Great ideas are often borne from two or more people standing firm on their ideas and opinions and trying to convince others to see it their way. When this happens, new ideas can emerge that might be better than any one individual had thought of previously.

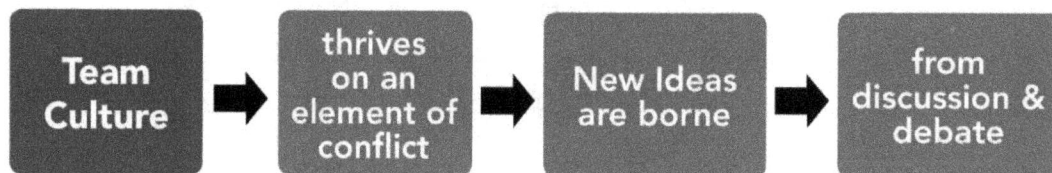

Team Culture → thrives on an element of conflict → New Ideas are borne → from discussion & debate

That healthy debate is often lost within a team that would rather pretend that they all agree for the sake of avoiding conflict and keeping everything friendly between team members. It is your job as manager to develop a culture that makes people comfortable with the idea of minor conflict in the name of learning and innovating. Striking a balance between healthy conflict and constant bickering is something that a good leader will need to do.

Lack of Commitment

Members of a team, no matter what the goal or task, need to be fully committed to the task at hand. Too often, people working within an organization don't really want to be part of the team they have been assigned to, so they end up faking their interest and concern for the team as a whole. Success is never going to be truly achieved when certain members of a team just aren't interested in giving their full effort to a project.

The solution to this problem is making sure that each member of the team understands how important their role is, and how important the project is as a whole. Most people naturally are going to be first concerned with what this means for them and their career, so identifying ways that each individual can personally benefit from the success of the team is a great way to improve 'buy-in' among the group.

Avoidance of Accountability

Within a team, there should be mutual accountability that helps to keep everyone moving forward toward a common goal. Not only should team members be accountable to the leader of the group, they should also feel like they are accountable to each other and themselves. This again comes back to ownership of the project and 'buying-in' to the process as a whole.

Standards should be high for any project that your team is engaged in. However, when no one is being held accountable properly for the work they are doing (or not doing), it puts everyone on a path toward poor performance and sub-standard work. Healthy teams will be able to hold each other accountable throughout the process and may not even need much from the leader in terms of motivation or management because they are successfully handling those functions among themselves.

Inattention to Results

The main objective should always be team success, not personal gain for either financial or ego purposes. While personal benefits can often be realized from being part of a successful team, the focus should start and remain on meeting the goals of the team first, with personal aspirations put on the back burner. When a team is made up of a group of individuals who are only focused on making sure that their individual needs and goals are met, the overall picture of the team is not likely to be a successful one.

These five 'Dysfunctions of a Team' are a great picture of what can go wrong within a team that has been built to work toward a specific goal. Any good manager will be able to watch out for signs of these problems so they can be mitigated as quickly and successfully as possible.

While it might not be realistic to try and avoid any of these issues altogether for the complete term of a project, maintaining a healthy team atmosphere as much as possible is desired. Teams that are able to mostly stay away from these five dysfunctions are ones that should be on a direct path for optimal performance.

Key Points

- ✓ The 'Dysfunctions of a Team' model by Patrick Lencioni addresses some of the common problems that are found within teams.
- ✓ Absence of Trust is simply having team members who are unwilling to trust each other, or their team leader.
- ✓ Fear of Conflict prevents the team from working through a healthy debate and arriving at new ideas that no one individual had thought of previously.
- ✓ Lack of Commitment means that success is unlikely to be achieved when certain members of a team won't give their full support to a project.
- ✓ Avoidance of Accountability means that no team member feels truly accountable for their work.
- ✓ Inattention to Results means that team members are focused on their own desires rather than the results being achieved by the team as a whole.
- ✓ Simply by understanding that these issues could exist within your team, you will be better prepared to identify and correct them as quickly as possible.

Birkinshaw's Four Dimensions of Management

Management is a complicated topic that takes on a variety of roles and functions within any organization. If you work as a manager in some capacity, you understand just how flexible you need to be in order to accomplish your objectives successfully.

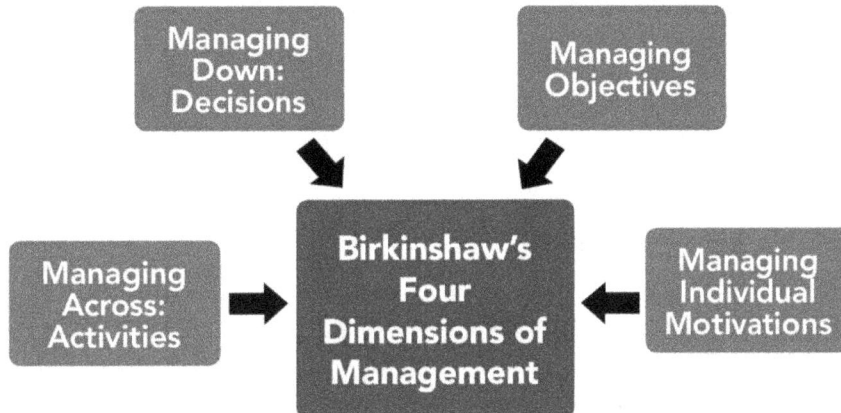

One of the challenges that comes with being a leader is deciding just how to go about your job and what management styles are going to be most successful for you in your organization. While some of your style is likely to be 'natural' to you, other parts of it you might have to work at until your find a method that you are comfortable with.

Birkinshaw's Four Dimensions of Management take a look at four different areas that managers need to deal with, and what kind of approach will work for each of them. Rather than offering up strict guidelines, this framework is meant to get you thinking about your own style and then to decide for yourself which way is going to be best.

The four dimensions are as follows -

1. **Managing Across: Activities**. This refers to lateral management of people that you don't necessarily have control over from a leadership perspective.
2. **Managing Down: Decisions**. This is more of what you think about when thinking of leadership—making decisions that affect a number of different people in different roles.
3. **Managing Objectives.** How are goals accomplished within the organization? There are a number of ways to chase down and accomplish various goals depending on what will work best for the leader and the team members.
4. **Managing Individual Motivation**. Possibly the most difficult part of leadership, keeping individual members of the team motivated from start to finish is crucial.

Within each of these dimensions, Birkinshaw offers two 'extremes' that form a scale for management style. Most organizations will fall somewhere within the limits of the scale, blending each of the styles that is represented on the far ends. One end of the scale is meant to represent the 'traditional' style of management', while the other is more 'alternative'. Let's look closer at each of these limits with the dimensions of management.

Managing Across: Activities

On one end of this dimension we have bureaucracy, and on the other end is emergence. As you would imagine, bureaucracy is the traditional form of management in this case.

With this style, most of the management is dictated by strict rules and guidelines that have been put in place to govern the whole organization. There is very little room for creativity or flexibility built in to a bureaucratic environment, but it can be effective when consistency is valued above all else.

Emergence is the opposite of bureaucracy, in that much of the power is put into the hands of the individual managers to be independent. Most people prefer working under these conditions as they are free to make Activities more choices and not live by the rules that have been set forth. However, emergence isn't going to be the best choice for all organizations as it could potentially lead to a chaotic feeling throughout the company.

Managing Down: Decisions

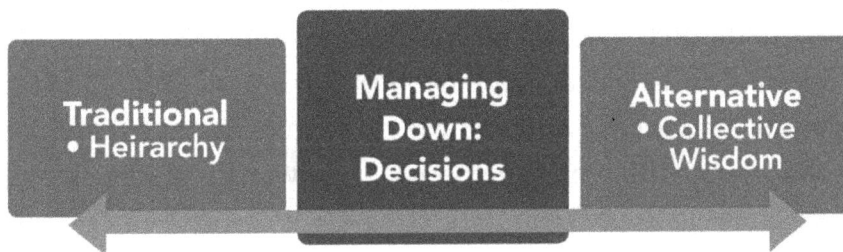

The two ends of the spectrum under this dimension are hierarchy and collective wisdom. Traditionally, hierarchy is the way that most organizations manage to make decisions. Authority trumps everything else in this situation, so the higher ranking person will win out in any disagreement or dispute.

This is the classic 'climbing the ladder' scenario, where employees put in their time early in their careers to later achieve management positions and the power that comes with them. Unfortunately, what can be lost in this style are the good ideas that those lower in the hierarchy might have to offer. Suppressing good ideas simply because of where they come from could hurt the organization in the long run.

The alternative to this style is collective wisdom, where everyone is welcome to help make decisions and offer up ideas. Naturally, those lower in the organization will appreciate this method, although it may discourage motivation to climb the ladder and achieve a position of power. Also, decisions can be slow and tedious to come by when there is input from so many different sources.

Managing Objectives

In this dimension, organizations will fall somewhere between alignment and obliquity. Alignment is the traditional method of goal setting, and the one that most managers tend to use because it is easily understood. Setting a specific financial goal or completion date for a project is an example of alignment, and then everyone on the team is tasked Managing with working specifically toward accomplishing that goal.

Obliquity, on the other end, is a less-direct method of goal setting. Instead of working toward that specific financial goal that the organization has in mind, the team will instead be given other goals that will hopefully lead the organization in the right direction as a result. Creativity is promoted under this style of management, as the team members have the freedom to chart their own path in terms of reaching the goals that have been set (or that they have set for themselves).

Managing Individual Motivation

Motivation can be a tricky thing to keep track of, let alone manage. Every individual is a different person, with different motivating factors in mind, and different goals for their life. The two ends of this scale are extrinsic and intrinsic. The most common motivating factor at work is extrinsic—usually meaning money. While a bonus or pay raise is usually the extrinsic motivation for getting the job done right, those motivators can also be negative, such as the threat of losing a job or being demoted.

Intrinsic motivation can actually be even more powerful than extrinsic, but it is harder to understand because it changes so much from person to person. While almost anyone will be motivated by the opportunity to earn more money, the things that motivate them intrinsically can be harder to pinpoint. What would be naturally motivating to one person might not be rewarding at all to another. Finding the right balance of motivating factors for each of your team members is an important part of management.

Key Points

- ✓ Birkinshaw's Four Dimensions of Management highlights four dimensions that represent key management processes and practices.
- ✓ Managing Across: Activities. This refers to lateral management of people that you don't necessarily have control over from a leadership perspective.
- ✓ Managing Down: Decisions. This is more of what you think about when thinking of leadership—making decisions that affect a number of different people in different roles.
- ✓ Managing Objectives. How are goals accomplished within the organization? There are a number of ways to chase down and accomplish various goals depending on what will work best for the leader and the team members.
- ✓ Managing Individual Motivation. Possibly the most difficult part of leadership, keeping individual members of the team motivated from start to finish is crucial.
- ✓ Within each of these dimensions, Birkinshaw offers two 'extremes' that form a scale for management style.
- ✓ You can use this model to help you to understand how best to manage the type of work that you're doing, and the values of your organization.

Waldroop and Butler's Six Problem Behaviors

Management would be a lot easier if everyone just behaved how you wanted them to at all times. Of course, that is a pipe dream. Management, and leadership, are the important roles that they are because people are hard to predict. Even when it isn't in the best interest of the team, or even themselves, employees often exhibit behaviors that you wish they wouldn't.

As a manager, it is your job to steer them back in the right direction without coming across as a dictator at the same time. It is a difficult balance to strike, but that is the challenge that you are given when you accept a leadership role.

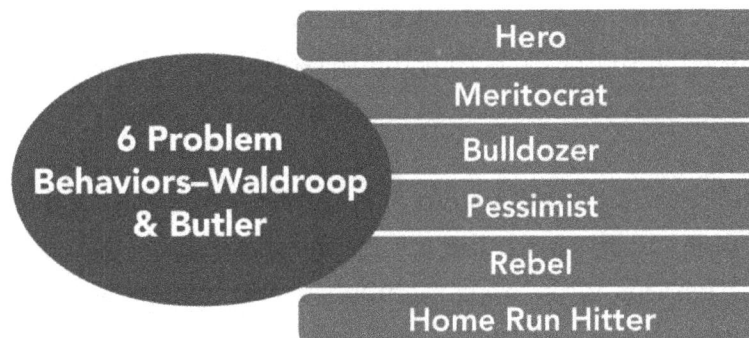

Waldroop and Butler have aimed to help managers everywhere by identifying six of these 'problem behaviours' along with their traits. When you see any of these six starting to become present in members of your team, taking quick action is the best option before their behaviour becomes a detriment to the group as a whole.

The Hero
The hero is an easy one to spot, and it might not seem like such a bad thing at first. This is the person who is going above and beyond what is expected to try and get the job done. However, there can be such a thing as trying too hard, and it can be detrimental in the end.

If you have a 'hero' personality on your team, you will need to watch out to make sure that they aren't burning themselves out—or burning out the people around them.

Naturally, this is a tricky situation as a manager, because the last thing you want to do is discourage them from achieving great things for themselves and for the organization.

Having conversations about good work-life balance is a place to start, just to make sure they understand that while you appreciate their efforts you are also concerned about their long-term career success.

The Meritocratic

Have you ever had a team member within your organization who felt like they were always right and didn't want to waste time explaining their decisions to you? That person would fall under the category of a meritocratic.

This problem behaviour is a challenge because this person feels like they are above the rest of the team, and their ideas should just be used without any discussion or debate. The difficulty here for a manager is that the person may in fact be right—so you don't want to squash their ideas just because of an abrasive personality.

However, for the betterment of the team as a whole, you will need to coach them into working more collaboratively with the rest of the team. Only when they are willing to engage in real discussions with other members of the group will their ideas really be welcomed and accepted.

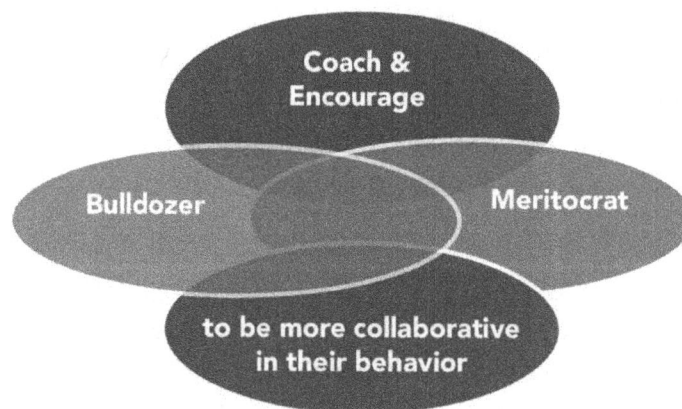

The Bulldozer

The profile of a bulldozer personality in the office isn't radically different from the meritocrat outlined above. As the name would indicate, the bulldozer is someone who is going to make enemies along the way just through their blunt and aggressive style.

Again, like the meritocrat, a bulldozer might be a valuable employee that brings plenty to the team—although they make everyone else angry at the same time. Being able to walk the line between this employee and the rest of the team is a challenge, so make sure to work with the person who is showing bulldozer tendencies and try to soften their approach a little bit.

The Pessimist

This one should need very little introduction. A pessimist on your team is going to think that every idea is a bad one, that every new initiative will fail, that there isn't enough time to finish, etc. This person can be harmful to the team because their negative attitude can spread and pretty soon the rest of the team will share this bad outlook. Even if the pessimist has good intentions and actually is a hard worker, their attitude alone can turn them into a liability within your group.

When dealing with this situation, it is important to get to know the person and figure out why it is that they are so negative in the first place. As long as they are willing to work on their outlook and try to see things from a more moderate perspective going forward, the pessimist could go on to remain a valuable member of the team.

The Rebel

There are certain people that just love to go against the grain. In some respects, the only thing they actually have a problem with is conformity itself. You might have one of these people within your team—called the rebel by Waldroop and Butler.

Dealing with a rebel is particularly challenging because it might not be clear exactly why they are complaining, or what they would like to see done differently. They do need to be addressed, however, because this kind of attitude can be counter-productive in terms of developing your team and reaching your goals.

Not everything about a rebel is a bad thing. Having people within your team who aren't afraid to challenge authority and who think for themselves is sometimes better than having a group of 'yes men'. When kept under reasonable control, someone with a slightly rebellious attitude can actually be an asset.

The Home Run Hitter

The final behaviour problem on the list is known as the home run hitter. As you would guess, this is a person who is always looking to make a big splash—even if they are overstepping their bounds or making choices that might not be in the best interest of the team as a whole. Patience is something that isn't usually exhibited by a home run hitter personality, so they may need to be coached into understanding their role as part of the team.

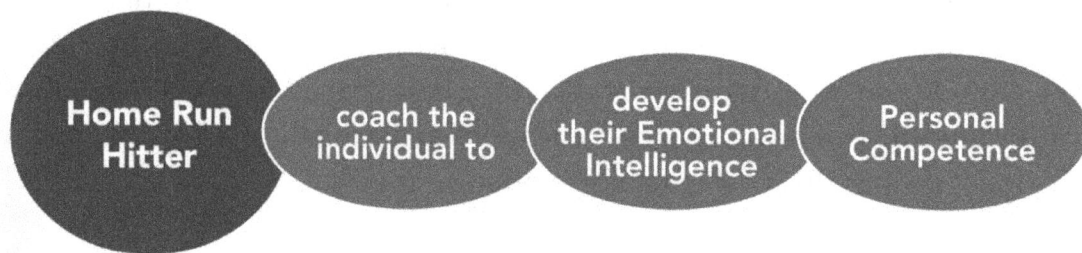

As with the hero personality, having home run hitters on your team can be a great thing as long as they have enough discipline and accountability to not push it too far.

Key Points

- ✓ Waldroop and Butler's Six Problem Behaviours model aims to help managers by identifying six of these 'problem behaviours' along with their traits.
- ✓ The behaviour patterns were assigned to six 'characters': the Hero, the Meritocrat, the Bulldozer, the Pessimist, the Rebel, and the Home Run Hitter.
- ✓ These characters have certain strengths that make them productive members of a team provided they are not allowed overdevelop.
- ✓ When you see any of these six starting to become present in members of your team, taking quick action is the best option before their behaviour becomes a detriment to the group as a whole.

Cog's Ladder

The development of a team is a process that takes time to come together successfully. Any manager who is even moderately experienced in leadership understands that you can't simply put a team together and expect them to work together perfectly right from the start. It takes time to grow into the roles that each person will fill, and for the group to gain momentum working in the right direction.

With that in mind, Cog's Ladder is a helpful tool to understand the development of any group. Published way back in 1972, Cog's Ladder is still highly relevant today and it is something that every manager should understand. There are five stages of group development highlighted as part of the 'ladder'.

Cog's Ladder of Group Development

5. Esprit

4. Co-operation

3. Power

2. Why are we here?

1. Polite

Polite Stage

This is the point in the process where the group is just getting started, and getting to know each other. As the name would indicate, the interactions between team members tend to be rather friendly at this point, and there are no major conflicts to be resolved. While this can be an enjoyable part of the process because it is low-stress and everyone is getting along nicely, it won't likely be the most productive part of the group's growth.

Once the members of the group become more comfortable with each other—and more willing to debate and stand up for their own ideas—productivity should benefit as a result. However, the polite stage is a necessary part of the development process because it lays the groundwork for what is to come. People who don't know, or trust, each other can't be expected to work together productively, so the polite stage gives them a chance to get to know one another and develop the trust that will be crucial later on.

Why we're Here Stage

Things are starting to 'come together' at this point in the process. Now that everyone is comfortable working together, some more specific goals and assignments can be set. While the group still might look more like a collection of individuals than a cohesive unit, it is starting to be more productive and get down to the business of doing whatever it was that brought them together in the first place.

Team members should have a much better understanding of their purpose and place on the team at this point as well. Successfully reaching this stage should position the team nicely for being successful in the stages ahead.

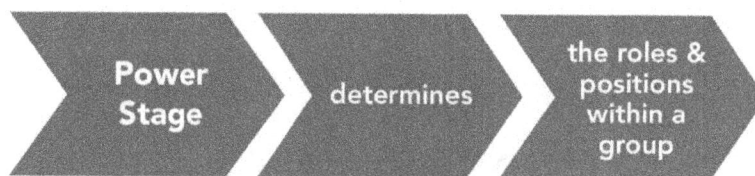

Power Stage

As the team develops and starts to evolve, the power stage is reached. This is the point where various members of the team are positioning themselves for leadership roles among the team, and conflicts start to arise. The conflict at this point in the process doesn't have to be a bad thing, as long as it is constructive in the end and ideas are being shared. The individuals that make up the team probably still don't feel 'connected' to the team concept, in large part because they are still battling for power and position with their peers.

What happens in the power stage will determine much of the rest of the team experience, as the roles become defined and people settle into their position as part of the group. Much of this can happen naturally without the direct input of the manager or leader. Even without appointing specific people to be in charge or leaders of portions of the group, those things will occur naturally through the course of day-to-day interaction.

Cooperation Stage

Finally, the group begins to really come together and work more as a unit than just a collection of individuals. Instead of having so many conflicts within the team, those conflicts turn into more of an 'us vs. them' situation, where the group battles against other parts of the organization. With the power battles mostly settled at this point, teamwork is greatly improved and the group as a whole is more accepting of new ideas and points of view.

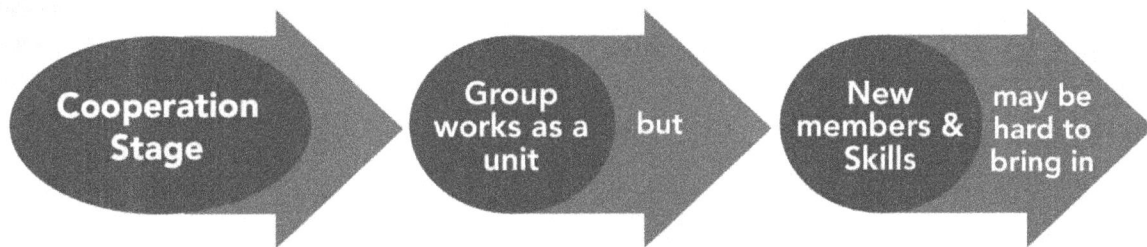

One negative effect of this stage is the difficulty that can be experienced when introducing a new member. The existing members of the team have successfully grown together by this point, and will likely resist having anyone added to their group at this point. While this does signify progress in terms of team building and camaraderie, it also can make it difficult to add a new skill set to the team when necessary.

Esprit Stage

Only successful groups will reach this final stage, but it should be the goal for every group that is formed within an organization. At this point, the team is working perfectly together and the goals of the individuals are put second behind the objectives of the team itself. The team starts to see itself as something of a family, and the members of the team trust each other completely when it comes to getting things done correctly.

As a benefit of the trust that exists, creativity may increase as members of the team are more comfortable taking chances and trying out new ideas. As a manager, it should be your goal to see your teams reach this level of cooperation and motivation. The results of this achievement can be powerful as the team may be able to do more than was ever expected when first starting out.

The development of each individual team that you create may vary slightly from time to time, but it should generally follow along this ladder. Understanding that teams take time to develop and evolve is important, and too much shouldn't be expected right from the start. As the team members gain experience working with each other, and build that trust that is so important, they will gradually come together more and more – and you can in turn expect more form the team in terms of production.

Understanding Cog's Ladder and what it means for the development of a group dynamic within your organization is a powerful tool that you can use to help get the most out of every individual, and the team as a whole.

Key Points

- ✓ The basic idea of Cog's Ladder is that there are five steps necessary for a small group of people to be able to work efficiently together. These stages are:
  - ✓ the polite stage,
  - ✓ the why we're here stage,
  - ✓ the power stage,
  - ✓ the cooperation stage &
  - ✓ the esprit stage.
- ✓ Cog's Ladder is very similar to Tuckman's Stages, another stage model of groups. Tuckman recognized 4 stages of team development:
  - ✓ Forming,
  - ✓ Storming,
  - ✓ Norming &
  - ✓ Performing.

Leader-Member Exchange Theory

One of the never-ending challenges associated with providing leadership is that we are all human and have our own biases and opinions. Even if you take pride in being a leader who is fair and you do the best you can to remain impartial and keep your personal feelings out of the equation, it is human nature to let yourself be swayed by emotion.

Dealing with certain team members in a different manner than others is a natural behaviour, but it is also one that could hurt the performance of your team in the long run. The Leader-Member Exchange Theory looks at this phenomenon and how your own personal opinions could end up limiting the opportunities that an individual has to succeed under your leadership.

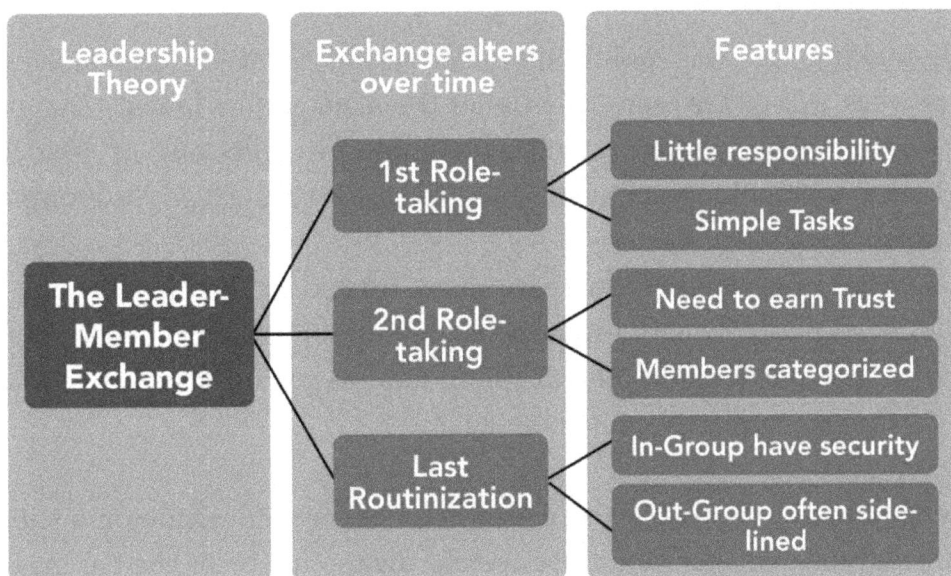

Leadership Theory	Exchange alters over time	Features
The Leader-Member Exchange	1st Role-taking	Little responsibility
		Simple Tasks
	2nd Role-taking	Need to earn Trust
		Members categorized
	Last Routinization	In-Group have security
		Out-Group often side-lined

While it might be difficult to look at yourself and your own management style in a critical light, it is important to do so from time to time. By taking an honest overview of what you are doing as a leader, and how you are treating all of your team members, you can improve your own performance over time—in addition to the performance of your organization.

Three Relationships

Throughout the progression of your time with specific team member, you are likely to work through three different 'relationships' with that person. Each of these stages is important, and takes time to develop naturally. If you think back to relationships that you have had with previous employees, you probably can identify these stages and remember how they developed over time.

- **Role-taking.** This is the very start of the relationship, when both the manager and the employee are just starting to get to know each other. Naturally, the employee won't bear very much responsibility at this point in the process, and their tasks will be relatively simple and limited in scope.

  It is during this period of time that the manager will be able to observe what the employee is capable of and then use that information to hand out future responsibilities.

- **Role-making**. At this point, the relationship is at its critical stage where employees will either earn the trust of the manager, or lose it—maybe forever. Most commonly, managers will put employees into one of two categories, without even thinking about it. These categories are called 'in-group' and 'out-group' in this theory.
  - Those who land in the in-group are trusted by the manager and are likely to increasingly earn promotions and further responsibilities.
  - Those pushed into the out-group tend to get stuck where they are, doing the same tasks over and over again.

It is important to note that these 'decisions' are usually made on a subconscious level, and the manager might not even be aware that he or she has grouped their employees in this way.

- **Routinization**. Finally, a routine is established in which the manager and employee generally know what to expect from each other.
  - This is good news for those who are in the in-group, as they will tend to remain in that position even if their actual performance isn't worthy of the position.
  - On the other hand, this is a bad thing for the out-group, as they are now going to have a hard time breaking the routine and impressing their manager.

Employees who fall into the out-group routine of doing the same thing day after day often end up leaving the group or asking for a new position within the organization to get away from the manager that has 'given up on them'.

What Can Be Learned

For a manager, the ideas put forward in this theory are important to recognize and consider. If there are subconscious decisions being made that are categorizing employees on potentially incorrect grounds, it could be compromising the overall potential of the group.

Ideally, the evaluation of employees would be strictly on concrete, objective grounds that leave personal feelings and opinions out of the mix. One of the best things any manager can do is look in the mirror critically and make sure that they are being fair to all of their employees to the best of their ability.

To learn from the Leader-Member Exchange Theory and actually improve performance, it is helpful to make sure and review every employee on a periodic basis and make sure that you are being fair to them — and that they are holding up their end of the bargain as well. By completing periodic reviews, you might find that you realize you haven't been giving a specific employee enough credit for the work they are doing, and that they deserve to be considered one of your top team members after all.

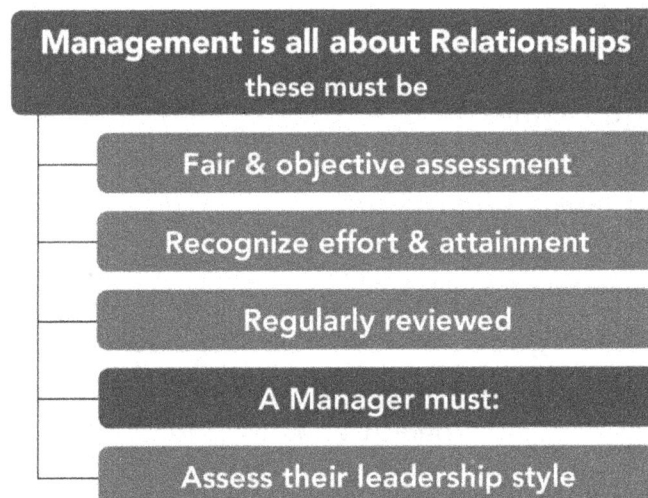

Management is all about Relationships
these must be

- Fair & objective assessment
- Recognize effort & attainment
- Regularly reviewed
- A Manager must:
- Assess their leadership style

On the other side of the coin, employee reviews are a powerful way to help you realize that some people on your team might not be as high achieving as you thought. This is often the case with someone who starts strong within the first few months of being on your team. That positive first impression can carry them a long way, even after they have stopped performing at such an impressive level.

If a particular employee figures out that they are on your 'good side', they might take advantage of the situation and let their performance slide, knowing that you are partial to them as compared to other members of the team. Just as those who are in your out-group deserve the chance to move up, those in the in-group need to be constantly evaluated to ensure that their reputation in your mind is warranted.

Being a manager is all about relationships, and those relationships inherently have human biases and flaws. By taking an objective look at each individual on your team from time to time, you can ensure that you are being fair to them and not pre-judging their work based on things that may have happened years ago in the early stages of their employment. Looking at your own leadership with a critical eye is an important skill, and the Leader- Member Exchange Theory can help you do just that.

Key Points

- ✓ The Leader-Member Exchange Theory looks at how your own personal opinions could end up limiting the opportunities that an individual has to succeed under your leadership.
- ✓ Throughout the progression of your time with specific team member, you are likely to work through three different 'relationships' with that person.
- ✓ Role-taking occurs when team members first join the group. Managers use this time to assess new members' skills and abilities.
- ✓ During Role-making managers sort new team members (often subconsciously) into one of two groups, known as the 'in-group' and the 'out-group'.
- ✓ During Routinization, routines between team members and their managers are established.
- ✓ A limitation of leader-member exchange research is that it is not particularly helpful in describing the specific leader behaviors that promote high-quality relationships as it only implies generalities about the need for leaders to show trust, respect, openness, autonomy and discretion.

Belbin's Team Roles

When looking at any team, it is quickly apparent that each member of the team adopts their own role in order to best contribute and use their skills in a way that is beneficial to the goals of the team as a whole.

Sports highlight this concept perfectly. On any sports team, whether it be football, basketball, baseball, etc., the players all have different positions. Each player is assigned a position, and the specific responsibilities that go along with that position. When a sports team is performing at a high level and winning their games, it is because all of the individual players are doing their jobs correctly and it is adding up to excellent performance.

It is a similar story for teams within any business organization. The members of such a team will either be assigned roles, or they will gradually take them on as time goes by. Teams who are able to successfully accomplish their goals on a regular basis usually have a healthy mix of the various team-roles that were identified by Dr. Meredith Belbin.

- People orientated roles
- Action orientated roles
- Thought orientated roles

These nine roles are grouped into three categories of three as shown in the diagram.

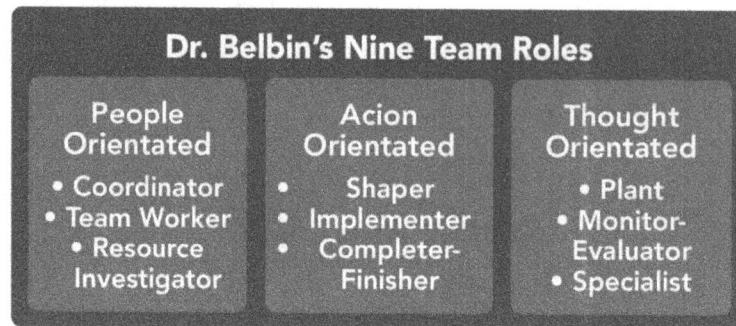

Dr. Belbin's Nine Team Roles

People Orientated	Acion Orientated	Thought Orientated
• Coordinator • Team Worker • Resource Investigator	• Shaper • Implementer • Completer-Finisher	• Plant • Monitor-Evaluator • Specialist

People Oriented Roles

These are roles that people take on who are generally good communicators, and enjoy working with others — either on the team, or from the outside.

- **Coordinator**. This person will take a leadership role within the team and be the person whom everyone else on the team feels like they can talk to when problems come up. Even if a higher-ranking manager is overseeing the project, most teams need someone like this to step up and lead the day-to-day activities of the group. Usually, this is a person that everyone on the team respects and will listen to.

- **Team Worker**. This is someone who really holds the group together, and is willing to sacrifice personal achievement or accomplishment for the better good of the team. Every good team will have at least a few people who fall into this category, although too many 'team players' on one team could be a bad thing as the team might lack the strong leadership needed to make decisions.

- **Resource Investigator**. Taking on the role of resource investigator is something that a person will do who is curious about new ideas and loves to think outside the box. Just like the previous two roles, this person is liked by the rest of the team and is comfortable with communicating with people on and off the team in order to get the answers and information that is needed.

Action Oriented Roles

Getting things done is what people who fall into this category are all about. Rather than being the ones to talk and discuss, these are the people who would rather get down to business and finish the job.

- **Shaper**. A shaper is someone who is going to take the lead on many projects and do their best to extract the best possible performance from the team. The status quo isn't going to be good enough for this person, and they don't mind being confrontational when necessary to see their vision come to life. While a team full of shapers could be in constant conflict, having at least a couple on the team is great for motivation and innovation.

- **Implementer**. Once there are ideas and plans in place, the implementer wants to get right to work bringing them to life. Communication might not be the strength of someone who fills this role, but they are absolutely essential to reaching milestones and completing projects. This person usually enjoys the challenge of the process, and will be detail-oriented in getting their job done right.

- **Completer-Finisher**. Someone on every team needs to be concerned with the small details at the end of a project, and that is the Completer-Finisher. Deadlines usually serve as strong motivation for this personality type, and others on the team may not appreciate their level of worry over getting everything done in a timely manner. However, a detail-oriented person is invaluable when it comes to confirming the quality of the work that is being completed.

People Roles
- Good communicators
- Like working with others

People Roles
- Perform tasks
- Accomplish goal

Thought Roles
- Innovators
- Seek new idea

Thought Oriented Roles

Ideas are the engine of any organization, and a company that stops having new ideas is one that will soon be in big trouble. Those people who fill the 'Thought' roles on a team are crucial to innovating and keeping the organization moving ahead.

- **Plant**. This is the creative person on the team, and the one who is always coming up with the latest and greatest idea. While the 'plant' role is vital on a team, this person might not always understand that some of their ideas aren't practical, and they won't necessarily work within the constraints that they have been given as far as timeline or budget.

- **Monitor-Evaluator.** It is probably best to think about this person as being one step away from a 'plant', in that they usually take the ideas that are generated within the team and then put them to the practicality test. Some ideas are great, and some are just not feasible, and the Monitor-Evaluator on the team will usually be the person to sort the good ideas from the others.

- **Specialist.** As the name would indicate, this is a person who has a specific skill set that plays a crucial role within the team. When something comes up that falls within their area of expertise they are ready to jump into action and take the lead. While specialization is their strength, it can limit their versatility and usefulness to the team when their particular skill is not in demand.

One of the first things that members of a newly-formed team need to do is figure out where they fall in with the rest, and what role they are going to take on. These roles usually develop naturally over time, depending on the makeup of the team and the specific task at hand. A good manager will observe the roles that are being filled on the team, and step in when necessary to balance out the composition of the group.

Key Points

- ✓ Belbin identified nine team roles and categorized them into three groups: Action Oriented, People Oriented, and Thought Oriented.
- ✓ Each team role is associated with typical behavioural and interpersonal strengths.
- ✓ He also defined characteristic weaknesses that tend to accompany each team role and referred to these as "allowable" weaknesses.
- ✓ A good manager will observe the roles that are being filled on the team, and step in when necessary to balance out the composition of the group.

Benne and Sheats' Group Roles

As a manager, you know just how complex and unpredictable teams and groups can be. Even when you have a group of highly qualified individuals with skills that are perfectly suited to the task at hand, you still might have trouble successfully reaching the goal. The problem, often, is that the personalities and roles that each person takes on might not successfully work together with the others in the group. Only when a team is comprised of a good balance of roles, along with the right skills, will it be successful.

Benne and Sheats' Group Roles are not new, but they are just as relevant now as they were when they were first published in the 1940's. There are a great number of roles that they defined, 26 in fact, and each of them is divided up into one of three categories— task roles, personal roles, and social roles. While we aren't going to go into each of the 26 roles here in this article, let's look at some of the more notable ones, along with the groups that they fit into.

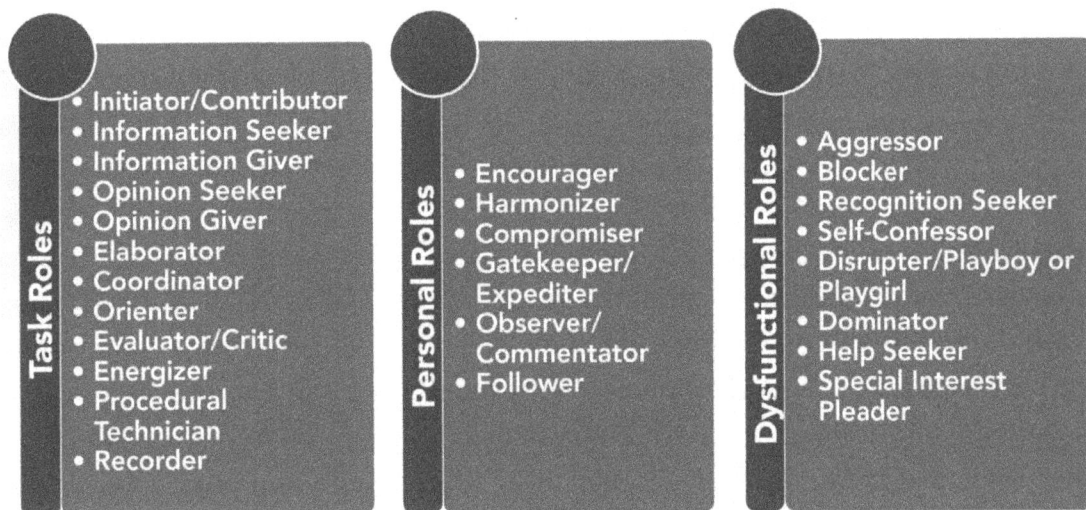

Task Roles
- Initiator/Contributor
- Information Seeker
- Information Giver
- Opinion Seeker
- Opinion Giver
- Elaborator
- Coordinator
- Orienter
- Evaluator/Critic
- Energizer
- Procedural Technician
- Recorder

Personal Roles
- Encourager
- Harmonizer
- Compromiser
- Gatekeeper/ Expediter
- Observer/ Commentator
- Follower

Dysfunctional Roles
- Aggressor
- Blocker
- Recognition Seeker
- Self-Confessor
- Disrupter/Playboy or Playgirl
- Dominator
- Help Seeker
- Special Interest Pleader

Task Roles

As the name would indicate, task roles relate to actually getting the job done. These are things that need to be completed along the path from getting a project started all the way through completion. One such role is that of the Information Seeker. This person tracks down all of the necessary information related to the project, and makes sure it is in place before getting too far along. This could mean bringing in additional people to the group that possess the necessary information, or simply doing some additional research.

Another member of the task roles group is the Elaborator. This role is important because this person generally will take the ideas of other people and expand on them until they are fully explored and considered. Sometimes, the ideas that an Elaborator works on will end up being dead ends—but other times they could turn into excellent options that the team as a whole needs to explore further.

A more outspoken member of the task roles group is the Opinion Giver. Never shy about speaking up, the Opinion Giver might rub some other people in the group the wrong way from time to time. However, this type of person is important because they may offer up ideas that no one else in the group had—or they were afraid to present. Groups are most successful when the individuals within them feel empowered to speak up and express their ideas, so an Opinion Giver can be a valuable asset.

One last vital member of the task roles group is the Energizer. No matter what kind of task or project is being worked on, there are bound to be periods of frustration or lagging motivation. The Energizer is the person that has a natural persistence and energy that can translate to the rest of the team. Staying motivated and focused on the goal is a big part of success in business, so this person can be indispensable on a group project.

Personal Roles
The interpersonal relationships within the group might have as much to do with its success or failure as any other single element. When people get along as part of a team, and respect each other as professionals, the results of a project are likely going to be much better. Unfortunately, it isn't always easy to get a group of people to work together toward a common goal—especially if that means temporarily putting aside their own personal aspirations or motivations.

The first role defined within this category is the Encourager. Much like the Energizer from the task roles category, this is a person who helps with morale and motivation. They have a positive attitude and generally get along well with everyone on the team. In the face of adversity, having at least a couple of people who naturally fill this role is a great benefit.

Along the same lines, the Compromiser is a welcome addition to a group for obvious reasons. Someone who fits in this role won't let their ego get in the way of compromising on a disagreement for the benefit of the team. Having too many Compromisers, however, could be troublesome as no one would be willing to take a stand and fight for their opinion.

Another quiet, but valuable, member of the team is the Follower. This person doesn't lead others in the group, but is happy to take direction and fill their role to the best of their ability. Many groups are undone by the fact that everyone wants to be in charge, so having a few Followers on the team is a necessary ingredient. While they may be quiet and even reserved, that doesn't mean their role on the team can't be crucial to success.

Dysfunctional Roles

A team is worse off for having any of these roles filled by one or more of its team members. Dysfunctional roles are those that don't serve any positive purpose and only further the frustration of the group. For example, the Aggressor is a classic example of a Dysfunctional role. This person is condescending with their comments to others in the group, and is usually trying to work their way to the top by knocking others down.

The Blocker is another example of someone who can hold a team back. This person doesn't like any of the ideas that are presented by other members of the group, yet never seems to offer up anything constructive on their own. With this person in the way, it becomes more difficult for the team to achieve its ultimate goals.

These are just a few examples from each category of the group roles defined by Benne and Sheats. For a manager, it is important to understand what kind of roles exist within a group so you can figure out who is playing what role on your teams. With that knowledge in hand, you can then make decisions with the goal of optimizing performance throughout the group.

Managers can also see how best to use individuals within the group so that changes in the working environment are quickly accepted and adaptations made. A team is unlikely to have all of these roles in separate individuals; managers usually find several of these behaviours within one person as they adapt to different circumstances. The key for any manger is to be aware of the types of behaviours they want to encourage and to minimize those that are dysfunctional.

Key Points

- ✓ Benne and Sheats' Group Roles were first published in the 1940's. These 26 roles are divided up into one of three categories — task roles, personal roles, and social roles.
- ✓ These role definitions are useful for looking at specific behaviours that occur within a group and evaluating it's current function and needs.
- ✓ They also provide a guide for team member development, as the more positive behaviours each person can display; the better able the whole group will be to respond to the demands put on it.

Margerison-McCann Team Management Profile

As any experienced leader will tell you, a good team is about more than just compiling the right people with the right experience and skills for the job. When done correctly, a team is more than the sum of its parts—a result of great teamwork and leadership that creates an environment of productivity and creativity. It is not the easiest task in the world to foster a healthy team setting, but it can be a powerful thing when it comes together correctly.

The Margerison-McCann Team Management Profile is a tool that organizations can use to help classify their employees in regard to what type of team member they are or will be. Using a set of 60 questions, this profile establishes some baseline information about each member of the team so that they can be placed into a specific spot on the Team Management Wheel.

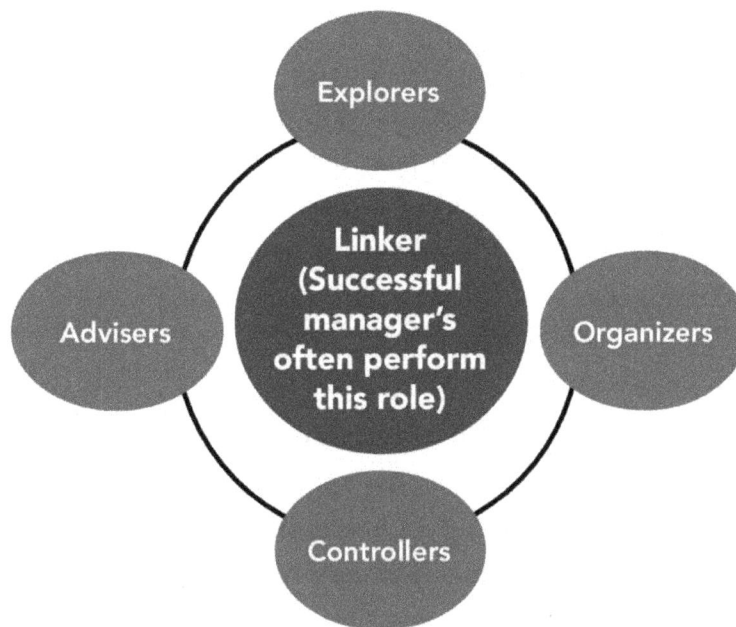

Using the analogy of the wheel the diagram above shows the different 'functional' areas around its circumference and that it must be 'linked' in its centre. The strength of a traditional wheel is made from the number of spokes it has. The more sections of the wheel that can be filled up by the members of a single team, the more complete that team will be.

The Team Management Wheel is made up of eight roles that make up the collection of spots on the 'wheel' within this theory. There is a spot at the center of the wheel, as well, which is considered a 'linker'. That means simply that there need to be some connection between the various roles around the wheel that brings them all together and allows the team to work as a unit.

While an ideal team would see a variety of team members successfully bring the unit together, often the leader will need to step in and serve as this person. If you are the manager of a team within your organization, one of the most important things you are going to need to do is serve as that link for the team members filling all of the various roles in your group.

There are eight 'role preferences' found on the wheel, and each is listed below with a short description. Starting with the adviser's section of the wheel and working clockwise around in explanation.

- Reporter/Adviser—is the person within the group who is adept at consolidating information and passing it out to the rest of the team. They want to make sure everyone is informed as much as possible so that they can make smart decisions with accurate information. Having a person like this on the team is important because it helps to keep the team working as a group instead of as a collection of individual employees.

- **Creator/Innovator**—is one of the biggest parts of the team. This is often the person that gets things going by presenting new ideas to the group that can be discussed and pursued further. One of the important elements to the group dynamic is that these kinds of people feel like they have the freedom to present their ideas in a welcoming and open environment. When the group dynamic is such that it restricts ideas and innovation, creativity often suffers as a result.

- **Explorer/Promoter**—role goes along somewhat with the previous category of Creator/Innovator. This is a team member that isn't just going to settle for the simple or basic plan—they are going to work toward new ideas and possibilities that might have been missed by the rest of the team. All good teams will have at least one person that fits into this category so they have the potential to rise above and beyond what is expected.

- **Assessor/Developer** — are people who are a little more interested in the practical side of the equation than the previous two roles. The Assessor/Developer likes to be on the cutting edge, but they are more motivated by putting things into motion and making them a reality than just the development of the idea itself.

- **Thruster/Organizer** — role within the team is someone who is helping keep progress moving and trying to reach completion as soon as possible. They will take the ideas and initiatives from other people within the group and work on making them come to life in an efficient and effective way. This is a person that usually gets satisfaction from seeing results of the work they have put in.

- **Concluder/Producer** — is an essential individual as one approaches the end of the project life cycle. They enjoy getting everything finished up nicely and out the door. While there isn't room on the team for everyone to fill this kind of a role, it is essential that someone does. Without a good Concluder at the end of the line to 'polish' everything up, all the good work that the team has done might be wasted because the product may never make it to market properly.

- **Controller/Inspector** — there are always plenty of small details involved in any kind of project, and it takes a special kind of person to be able to handle those details and be motivated by that kind of work. The person that fits into the Controller/Inspector spot on the wheel is necessary because they will pick up on small points that others have missed along the way and make sure those things get taken care of.

- **Upholder/Maintainer** — the last role on the Team Management Wheel is that of the Upholder/Maintainer. This is the type of person who wants to not only make sure that everything is getting done, but that it is getting done correctly as well. They value their spot on the team and want to see the team as a whole be as successful as possible no matter what project is currently taking place.

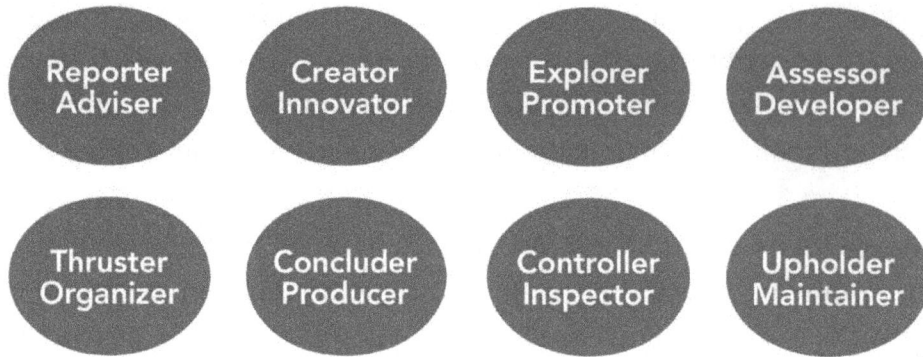

The eight roles above make up the collection of spots on the 'wheel' within this team management theory. It is certainly possible to get a group of people to work together successfully on a project, but it can be a challenge. It takes more than just experience working in a specific field—it takes a good blend of personality types, and the willingness of the team members to buy-in to the overall project and come together as a unit. When this happens, great things are possible for both the group and the organization as a whole.

Key Points

- ✓ The Margerison-McCann Team Management Profile is a tool that organizations can use to help classify their employees in regard to what type of team member they are or will be.
- ✓ Using a set of 60 questions, this profile establishes some baseline information about each member of the team so that they can be placed into a specific spot on the Team Management Wheel.
- ✓ The more sections of the wheel that can be filled up by the members of a single team, the more complete that team will be.

The JD-R Model

In the JD-R Model, the 'JD' refers to job demands, while the 'R' refers to resources. The idea behind this model is all about making sure managers and leaders within an organization have everything they need to meet the demands of their job. Despite the fact that managers are often in some of the most high-stress positions within an organization, this model promotes the theory that much of that stress can be taken away when monitored properly.

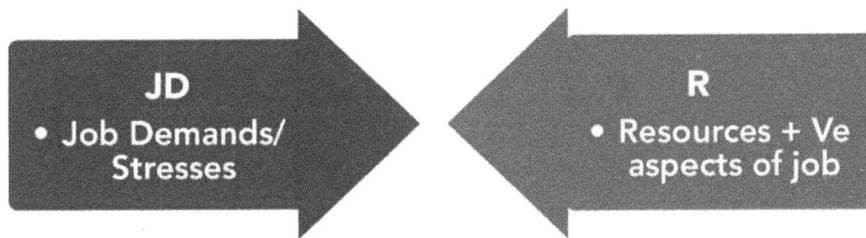

In this context, the researchers of this study (Bakker and Demerouti) are using the word 'resources' to highlight the positive aspects of the job that counteract the stress that the demanding part of the job place on the individual. For example,

If a manager has a high level of responsibility and faces many time-sensitive deadlines, they may also need some additional time away from the office or another perk to balance out that stressful demand.

This kind of give and take relationship within the model can take on many different real- world manifestations. The visual representation of this model is divided up into four quadrants, each of which demonstrates a different state for the manager in question depending on the resources and demands that they are experiencing.

- Low Demands/Low Resources—in the bottom left quadrant, we find the employee who isn't being asked to do too much, but also doesn't have much to feel rewarded by. They certainly aren't overworked at this point in time, but they also might be suffering from a lack of motivation due to the low level of resources available to them. Getting burned out isn't a fear at this point in the model, but high levels of performance seem unlikely.

- High Demands/Low Resources—is probably the worst position to find yourself in throughout the entire model. At this point, the employee is dealing with a great number of stresses—things like tight deadlines, a shrinking budget, conflict with others, etc. However, they aren't receiving the resources they need to counteract this problem and get it corrected quickly.

  A person in this position is very likely to burn out, and may just quit completely due to too much stress. Every organization should strive to avoid placing their employees or managers in this quadrant of the model.

		Job Demands / Stresses	
		Low	High
Resources / +Ve Aspects	High	Low Strain Average Motivation	Manageable Strain High Motivation
	Low	Little Strain Lack of Motivation	High Strain Close to burn out

- Low Demands/High Resources—on the opposite side of the coin, this is likely the best place to find yourself within the model. This employee has everything they need to get their job done correctly, and they aren't feeling a high level of strain from the pressures of their work. There is no reason that this person shouldn't be feeling content with their job, and motivated to go on and achieve even more. For an organization, getting as many employees as possible into this section of the JD-R Model is the ideal outcome.

- High Demands/High Resources—finding yourself in this spot is not the worst thing that can happen at work, but you might be feeling the strain of all of your job stress anyway. People who are at this point on the model are likely to be somewhat stressed, yet they still may be happy with their job because of all the resources they have available to them—and the opportunities that could still be to come. Even though they can be feeling the pressure, most people in this situation are still highly motivated because they can see the possibility of better things coming down the road.

Every employee within an organization should be able to be fit into one of those four categories above. The more people who feel like they have plenty of resources and relatively low demands that are within the business, the better off that business is likely to be. A high stress, low resource work environment is the worst possible case, and that organization will likely see plenty of turnover as employees look for better opportunities.

Making a Change

When a company does find that many of their employees feel they are in the high demand/ low resource portion of the grid, there are some steps that can be taken to alleviate the problem. The first is to determine why the employees feel the level of stress that they do, and what can be done about it. While some stress comes along with working, too much can be a damaging thing for both the individual, and the company. Upper management should look at ways to reduce these stresses so that the majority of employees feel better about their situation.

Some of the things that could be causing high levels of stress include not giving employees enough time to finish their work, not providing any opportunities for advancement or raises, or simply not providing work that is interesting or challenging in some way. An organization might not be able to remove all of these issues, but even addressing them and working with the employees together to improve conditions can go a long way.

Of course, the other end of the spectrum is providing employees with more resources to counter those stresses that they do deal with. There are a number of ways in which this can be done. Some of those include providing plenty of training and job support from higher-ranking managers, more freedom to do the work as the employee sees fit, and better advancement opportunities that provide a clear career path.

You will likely find that some of these options work great to motivate and help some employees, while other employees are interested in different resources. Only by offering a range of resources and benefits to your team members will you be able to get all of the employees the assistance they need.

Key Points

- ✓ The Job Demands-Resources (JD-R) Model states that when job demands are high and job resources/positives are low, then both stress and burnout increase.
- ✓ Increasing the positive aspects of a job can offset the effects of high job demands. Identify and promote the job positives that act as a buffer between your team members and the demands of their roles.
- ✓ These can include: Mentoring or coaching, training and development, regular constructive feedback, and increased autonomy.

Summary

Keeping everyone within your organization happy and motivated is a lofty goal, but a worthwhile one at the same time. These ten leadership models offer you a variety of ways to assess the capabilities, commitment and compatibility of your team members. They can also help you better understand your own leadership style and its impact on those you manage.

It is important to remember that an organization is only as good as the people that it employs, and your people are only going to be at their best when they feel comfortable with their roles and supported by the organization. Give them what they need to succeed, and they will usually reward you with excellent performance.

Team Briefing Checklist

Your team brief provides you with a perfect opportunity to communicate with your team and gauge their level of motivation and satisfaction. This checklist walks you through the process of preparing a team brief so that they are seen as effective and informative

Actions

1. Be aware of and follow any guidelines for team briefs that your organization has. But ensure that deliver the brief in your own style so that it comes across as real desire to communicate with your team members and reflects the type of team you are responsible for.

2. Set your team's expectations of the team brief by explaining your objective of this meeting and the type of behaviour and communication you expect, for example
   - o Hold questions till the end of each agenda item.
   - o This is the opportunity for the team to have open and honest exchange of information and ideas.
   - o Attendance is expected for all.

The actual location you are able to hold such a briefing in may dictate the extent to which you are able to have an open exchange, but if possible it needs to be away from the team's desks to ensure you have their full attention.

3. Depending on the nature of your role within the organization you may have to have a series of cascade team briefs to communicate with your whole team. Whatever style of your briefs you need to:

   Diarize the time, date and location of your team briefs for at least six months or the whole year. Be mindful of the different work patterns of your team e.g.
   - o Mixture of full and part-time workers.
   - o Shift and rotation workers

   If you need to delegate this task to department or divisional heads give them clear guidelines on how to achieve your objective for such meetings.
   - o Optimum size of briefings s 4-12 people.

4. Create a broad timed agenda for your team briefs so that everyone knows what to expect. Any one-off items can be added as needed and communicated prior to that meeting.

Agenda example:

Corporate Update	5mins
Division/Department Update	10mins
Team/Project Update	15mins

Write short notes to remind yourself of all key points you want to communicate. Where possible end the meeting on a positive note. Avoid using technical jargon or acronyms that will be unfamiliar to your team.

5. Prepare yourself for the likely concerns and questions your team will bring up during the briefing.

Where you need to seek further information or advice to answer a question or concern make sure that you inform those at the briefing when you will get back to them.

This feedback should take place as quickly as possible. If the timeframe forces a response to be longer than a week communicate the progress you have made in obtaining an answer.

Team Leadership Checklist	
Behaviour That Emulate Successful Leaders	**Identify your own Instances of these Behaviours**
Define success criteria 1. Define and communicate your team's objective in a way that is easily understood by everyone. 2. Allow everyone in the team the opportunity to contribute in this process, regardless of their skill or expertise. 3. Ensure any success criteria are set at realistic levels, in this way the whole team will be able to 'buy into' them. **Remember, success can only be achieved if the team knows what it looks like.**	
Lead by example 1. You must exhibit the same professional behaviours to everyone you interact with, whether they are in or outside of your team. 2. Demonstrate the behaviours you expect from your team in all your own interactions. 3. Ensure that you allocate time to communicate and monitor your team informally Contact time with your team will enable to more easily pick up on underlying issues and resolve them before they become serious.	

Behaviours That Emulate Successful Leaders	Identify your own Instances of these Behaviours
Value all contributions 1. Show that you value each member's views of a situation regardless of their role. 2. Ensure all views are heard and acknowledged by actively listening during meetings or discussions. 3. By your example ensure viewpoints are well presented. **Avoid your team fragmenting by making certain everyone feels involved and valued**	
Reward success 1. Recognize an individual's or sub-teams contribution to the project or objective, both to the individual, the team and senior management. 2. Reward this achievement success as best you can within your ability to make such decisions of this nature and your organization's culture. **It is key that any recognition you give is in proportion to the achievement attained.**	

TEAM DEVELOPMENT CHECKLIST

This free checklist shows you the behaviours your team requires you to exhibit during its four-stage development. By successfully supporting your team as it evolves you will have a high performing group that displays trust, expertise and cohesion.

STAGE 1 - FORMING

- You need to adopt a hands-on approach to management and support for your team.
- All your communications must be clear, concise and use appropriate language for your team.
- You must provide a structure for the team and guidance as they perform their role.
- Your aim is to build good relationships within the team.

STAGE 2 - STORMING

- You need to control the conflict that will result as differences are expressed and worked out by actively listening to exchanges between members.
- Offer the support the team need at this stage of their development rather than guidance.
- Your role is to aid and offer explanation for the decisions made.
- You may need to alter the composition of the team so that is can operate effectively.

STAGE 3 - NORMING

- During team performance of tasks and discussion your role is one of observer so that trust and cohesion can develop.
- Your purpose is to facilitate team members in their decision-making process so that an environment of harmony and team pride is created.
- Your role becomes one of a mentor and delegator offering your team greater opportunities for raising their levels of expertise.

STAGE 4 - PERFORMING

- As manager your role now is one of a delegator, briefing your team thoroughly and in sufficient detail and enough resources that they can achieve their objective.
- You are able to oversee you team as they work towards their goal because they are now competent and autonomous in handling the decision-making process.
- It is essential you monitor your team's relationships and performance to ensure that the group dynamics remain positive and productive.

PERFORMANCE IMPROVEMENT CHECKLIST

This checklist will help guide you through the steps you need to take to address any underperformance from your team.

Remember this will not happen over-night it takes time to re-establish good working relations within your team.

YOUR BEHAVIORS	
Communications	One of the most important aspects of any team is how it communicates. This is between its members and with those outside of the team. Communications must be two-way, open and honest. When communicating with your team you must: • Be specific and detailed when making a request. • Use the appropriate level and content of language. • Check for understanding. • Sum up goals in a way team can buy into
Goals	When defining the goals of the team and its members you must: • Clearly state the objectives you wish to achieve. • State the priorities assigned to different tasks. • Set each member and the team SMART goals that are motivating. • Through the appraisal process ensure that you develop each individual through a mixture of Coaching, Mentoring and Training.
Rapport	You can only establish a good working rapport with your team members if you: • Have open and honest communications. • Gain the trust of each member of the team. • Restore the self-esteem of your members.
Lead by Example	Show your team the KSA's (Knowledge, Skills & Attitudes) and behaviors you require from them by: • Supporting and helping members resolve issues. • Avoid blame to solve problems • Your interactions with other team members • Your attitude & Interactions with those outside of the team and organization.

	STEPS REQUIRED TO ADDRESS POOR PERFORMANCE
1. Know your team's history	Look at previous appraisal forms to: • Gain an appreciation of each members performance and their KSA's • Ascertain each person's development plan. • What training an individual has received and how its been used in their role, if at all. • Level of coaching and mentoring that has been offered to each team member. • Personally talk and make you own assessment of each individual, comparing this to what has been documented.
2. Get to know each individual	Through open and honest communications with each team member make your own assessment of their level of: • Self esteem. • Satisfaction. • Motivation. • Aspirations.
3. Build rapport & trust through Appraisal process	Rebuilding the rapport with management takes time and consistency. To attain this you need to conduct: • 360° evaluations for each team member at different levels appropriate to your team's role: • By team itself, • Others within organization interact with, • Outside contacts the team members have dealings with. • Appraisals for each person. • Set SMART goals to motivate members • Offer real coaching and mentoring to develop individuals • Use delegation to develop members KSA's with your support • Agree & deliver training to develop each person's KSA's
4. Reward good performance	Ensure an individual receives the recognition that was outlined at the start of a task once completed successfully. You need acknowledge this: • Personally • Within the team • Rest of organization • Where appropriate externally

	Reward good performance within the constraints of your role & that culture of the organization • Informal – e.g. cakes for team • Formal – bonus, meal on expenses, time off in lieu etc.
Performance improves as trust and self-esteem are restored within the team.	

Team Productivity Template

You can quickly assess your team's productivity by using the basic principles of Pareto's analysis. This will give you a framework of information that you then have to prioritize how you deal with in terms of practical solutions and the current working environment.

STEP 1 – LIST PROBLEMS & IDENTIFY THEIR CAUSES (most likely)

Dates	Problem that Occurred	Cause of Problem	Is Cause Always the same?
			Yes / No
			Yes / No
			Yes / No
			Yes / No
			Yes / No
			Yes / No
			Yes / No

STEP 2 – IDENTIFY RE-OCCURRING CAUSES & RATE LEVEL OF IMPACT ON PRODUCTIVITY			
Re-Occurring Cause	Number Problems it Created	Which Problem (s) it Created	Rate Level of Impact
1.			HIGH MED LOW
2.			HIGH MED LOW
3.			HIGH MED LOW
4.			HIGH MED LOW
5.			HIGH MED LOW
6.			HIGH MED LOW
Impact on Overall Team Productivity (circle):		HIGH/IMPROVING/ADEQUATE/DECLINING/POOR	

STEP 3 – GROUP CAUSES BY LEVEL OF IMPACT & A POTENTIAL SOLUTION			
HIGH Impact Causes	Potential Solution	Actions Required & Deadline	Owned By

MEDIUM Impact Causes	Potential Solution	Actions Required & Deadline	Level of Urgency	Owned By
			HIGH MED LOW	
			HIGH MED LOW	
			HIGH MED LOW	
			HIGH MED LOW	

Low Impact Causes	Potential Solution	Actions Required & Deadline	Level of Urgency	Owned By
			HIGH MED LOW	
			HIGH MED LOW	
			HIGH MED LOW	
			HIGH MED LOW	

TEAM SATISFACTION TEMPLATE														
For each team member you need to assess how satisfied they are with each of Herzberg's hygiene factors. Use their initials in each column and those individuals with a high score are the most dissatisfied and require you to act to rectify to prevent this sentiment spreading within the team. SCALE of 1=Very Content/2=Partially Satisfied/ 3=Satisfied/ 4=Minor Issues / 5=Dissatisfied														
Individuals Initials														
Salary														
Benefits														
Job Security														
Working Conditions														
Relationships with You														
Level of supervision,														
Relationships with co-workers														
Organizational policies & procedures														
TOTAL FOR EACH INDIVIDUAL														
You need to regularly revisit and update this form to prevent dissatisfaction because Hygiene Factors are cyclical in nature and the 'Norm' is constantly being adjusted to incorporate new changes within it.														

Attributes	Level Of Proficiency		Identify Areas of Improvement	Required Actions	Deadline
	Current	Desired			
Satisfy internal clients	HIGH MED LOW				
Satisfy external clients	HIGH MED LOW				
Develop future capabilities as part of the team activities	HIGH MED LOW				
Members find meaning and satisfaction within the team	HIGH MED LOW				

TEAM IMPROVEMENT TEMPLATE

This template enables you to identify areas in which your team can improve both for members and the team as a whole.

Attributes	Level	Potential Improvement	Required Actions	Deadline
Stability of group members	High/Med/Low			
Level of member turnover	High/Med/Low			
Integration of new members	High/Med/Low			
SMART goals for members	Yes/ No			
Members know how they contribution to organization	Yes/ No			
Size of team	Too Big / Okay			
Variation of tasks	High/Med/Low			
Social Skills	Good/Ok/Poor			
Support Through				
Reward	High/Med/Low			
Development	High/Med/Low			
Information	High/Med/Low			
Ability to Offer				
Coaching	Yes/Partial/No			
Mentoring	Yes/Partial/No			
Training	Yes/Partial/No			

References

- Hackman, J.R. and Wageman, R. (2005), 'When and How Team Leaders Matter,' Re- search in Organizational Behaviour.

- Harrison, D.A. and Klein, K. (2007), 'What's the Difference? Diversity Constructs as Separation, Variety, or Disparity in Organizations,' Academy of Management Review, 32.

- Katzenbach, J.R. and Smith, D.K. (1993), The Wisdom of Teams: Creating the High-perfor- mance Organization, Boston: Harvard Business School.

- Lewis-McClear, Kyle and Taylor, M.S. (1998), 'Psychological Contract Breach and the Employment Exchange: Perceptions from Employees and Employers.' Paper Presented to the Academy of Management, San Diego, August 1998.

- Mello, A.S. and Ruckes, M.E. (2006), 'Team composition,' Journal of Business.

- MIT Information Services and Technology (2007), Guide for Creating Teams: Definition of Teams.

- Tuckman, Bruce (1965), 'Developmental Sequence in Small Groups,' Psychological Bul- letin 63.